MW00945602

Backstage Shenanigans

Memoirs of a Wardrobe Mistress

Trina Greig

ISBN: 1512056766
ISBN-13: 978-1512056761

DEDICATION

For my family and friends who motivated me to publish the stories of my theater days.

Trina Grieg 1925–2014

CONTENTS

ACKNOWLEDGMENTS

Although Trina has passed on, I know she would like to thank the La Mesa Creative Writer's group in California for giving her feedback on her writing and encouraging her to publish hr wonderful stories. Her memoirs as a wardrobe mistress and seamstress in the early off-Broadway theater days of San Diego entertained and made us laugh out loud. A special thanks to Daniel Henderson who read her stories aloud to get them into a digital format, to Maureen Brown who did the book layout to get it ready for publishing, and to Linda Payne Smith who edited and helped fill in wherever it was needed to publish the book for Trina's family, friends and those who love the theater.

I Become a Mistress

"Hi, Trina, glad to meet you. Shall I take my pants off now?"

That was my introduction to Dana Andrews, "the" Dana Andrews. Tall, still handsome, with thick wavy gray hair, there he stood —in baggy white boxer shorts!

Some of my illusions were shattered, but I took out my measuring tape and tried to look as if I saw famous people in their underwear every day.

I had recently become the wardrobe mistress for a small theater. *Plaza Suite*, the play Dana was starring in, was only my second show and I was still pretty green. I eventually got used to the unblushing nudity and colorful language of professional actors. I even learned to measure the inseam of men's' trousers without turning scarlet, but that took a while. In the meantime I had a lot to learn.

Did you ever wonder, when watching a play, about where the costumes came from? I learned that—the hard way.

I have never been a brave person. In fact, anyone unkind would probably call me a coward. I shake inside when I'm introduced to someone new, my hands sweat if I have to talk on the telephone, and vacuum cleaners, washing machines – even typewriters defy me. I can sew, and sew well, but just let me sit down in front of that monster – the sewing machine – and it has my number immediately. It senses my fear and deliberately loosens its nuts and bolts, breaks needles, and smears things with oil.

I have sewed since I was a child but each new piece of

fabric fills me with dread. The scissors wobble in my clammy hands, the pins slip, and the pattern instructions are suddenly written in Swahili.

My friends try to help. "You're so good," they say. "You have a real talent. You can do anything!" But they're my friends. They tell me that to make me feel good. My enemies don't say anything. I don't give them the chance. I spent my life avoiding anyone who doesn't think I'm great.

I've even tried self-hypnosis. "You are good," I told myself. "You have a real talent. You can do anything!" I did succeed in putting myself to sleep and woke up convinced that, along with all the rest of my faults, I was also a terrible liar.

These faults combine to make me somewhat less than the perfect person to be the Wardrobe Mistress in a theater. A wardrobe mistress has to meet a complete new cast of actors every few weeks. She spends hours on the telephone trying to borrow and beg things from friends, foes, stores, and other theaters. She has to sew—and fast. There's no time to be afraid of the sewing machine because she is usually given only about seven days to get a show put together. I accepted the job in what must have been a moment of total insanity.

I needed work.

Arthritis had recently put an end to my thirty years as a ballet teacher and choreographer. I was untrained for anything else, and when one is afraid of people, new situations, mechanical things, the dentist, and even old Japanese horror movies, one is not very good job material.

When an old friend called and told me a new theater was opening that needed a wardrobe mistress, I said I couldn't possibly do it, had never been a W. M., etc. But the O.F. was stubborn and talked me into applying.

4

They must've been desperate— I was hired.

It certainly sounded easy enough. I would be expected to be at the theater every night except Monday and for Saturday and Sunday matinees. It would be my responsibility to keep the wardrobe clean and mended. The costumes all had to be rented so what could go wrong? I shook hands with my new boss, a nice little round man, (directors' horns never show until rehearsals are underway) got kissed on both cheeks by the set designer (set designers are rather given to that sort of thing) and I was a wardrobe mistress.

I was delighted with the theater itself. Originally an old burlesque house, it had been redecorated with reddish carpets and crystal chandeliers. It was a small, intimate theater complete with a balcony, side boxes, and red velvet curtains. Backstage all the dressing rooms—two upstairs and five down—had been beautifully carpeted and painted. There were lots of lights, mirrors, and new chairs, each with four legs that stuck out like large monster claws, perfect for banging toes against and tripping over. I heard more raunchy language because of those chairs than I ever did about anything else, even salaries.

No two downstairs dressing rooms were the same size. Numbers1 and 3 would hold three people if they were very friendly. Number 5 was a bigger room, but because of the crazy way it was built, would only hold two, comfortably. Number 2 was the big one. It was intended for eight actors, but sometimes when we did a musical there'd be as many as twelve. Number 4 was only large enough for one person and so cold it was only used for dressing when there wasn't any place else.

Besides, it was haunted.

When I first heard the stories about the theater ghost and how people had been for many years getting glimpses of him, a tall, thin man, I thought everyone was joking. Admittedly there was a cold draft that often blew through the small room, but I pointed out that the air conditioning unit was there and probably had something to do with it.

I couldn't fight the superstition. Somehow the word always got around to each new cast and often, if Number 4 had been assigned to anyone, he or she would soon find some excuse to move into Number 2. It was big, light, and usually full of people.

I spent many nights alone in the theater – I lived out in the country and sometimes there wasn't time to drive home and back, so I'd sleep for a few hours in the big dressing room where there was a folding cot.

Sometimes the crew would be working upstairs all night to get the new set finished and it was comforting to know I wasn't alone. Once in a while I'd have the place to myself. The ghost never bothered me—or I was too tired to hear him prowling. I realized, though, before too long, that I, too, was gradually avoiding dressing room number four.

The theater was beautiful, but there wasn't any room for me. No one had even thought about a place for the wardrobe mistress. The only place downstairs that wasn't being used was a small cubbyhole at the bottom of what had been a flight of stairs leading into the auditorium. It had been blocked off and cemented over, leaving seven concrete steps and a five by seven space between them and the water heater.

Well, it wasn't much, but it was to be mine, so I built my nest there.

The boys on the stage crew volunteered for duty. They found a rickety table in the warehouse and fixed it so it would hold my sewing machine. They built shelves, made me a bulletin board, and cleaned the debris off the steps so I could use them as storage space. By the time I got an ironing board set up there was only enough space to turn around in, but it was cozy, and the actors used to sit on the steps and chat with me.

I'm not the best housekeeper in the world and my small space usually looked like a disaster area – but I knew where everything was – the mending tape, the extra black socks, the shoe polish, aspirin, razor blades, Tums, Kleenex, mouthwash, nail polish, shirt collar stays, shoe-strings—all the paraphernalia a good wardrobe mistress must have on hand.

My bulletin board was originally for cast lists and important notices, but was soon covered with a conglomeration of things that I didn't want to throw away and couldn't find any other place for. Those, in turn, were eventually covered, as was my whole wall, with my "rogues' gallery," the signed photographs of all the people I've worked with. How I prize those pictures and the beautiful sentiments written on each one.

Recently I noticed the edges of the pictures were curling so I took them down to back with cardboard. Underneath, pinned to the bulletin board I found a swastika cut out of thin foam rubber, two artificial hat roses, a long red feather, three big hat pins that I'd been looking for, for weeks, a piece of the Santa Claus beard, an MP armband, a very dead rose (once a live opening night gift,) seventeen scraps of paper with names and addresses of people I had intended to correspond with, four lists I'd put up at different times, a black mink tail, a blue satin G-string, and, a red sequin pastie. If you're not familiar with G-strings and pasties, well, I wasn't either, but I learned when we did *Lenny*. I'll tell you this much. They're worn by strip teasers and in burlesque shows, leave little to the imagination, and are a damn nuisance to make.

But, I digress. Back to the theater itself. There was one big point on the debit side. Our small jewel was set right in the middle of the worst part of town. Surrounded by gaudy bars, massage parlors, "adult" bookstores, twenty-five cent peep shows and drab hotels. It would take a miracle (and thousands of publicity dollars) to bring theater-goers to that vicinity.

Miracles do happen.

We opened with a gala performance of *Anything Goes*, starring Dorothy Lamour and Sterling Holloway. There were pretty dancing girls, handsome young actors, elegant sets and costumes, Klieg lights, champagne, and a busload of celebrities from Hollywood. The show went beautifully, the critics and cast happy the San Diego off-Broadway theater was launched.

And the program read—Wardrobe Mistress—Trina Greg."

Anything Goes—And Almost Did

Having been assured that the costumes for our first show, *Anything Goes* had all been rented, and altered to fit the actors, I entered the theater on my first day with, for me, quite a bit of confidence. I was shaky about meeting the director and the actors, but managed to deceive everyone with my (outward) professionalism. Everyone seemed to take it for granted that I'd been a wardrobe mistress for years so I just let them believe it. Having been a dancer and a part-time actress myself, I was able to put on a good show—even when the actors started coming to me one after another with costume problems.

The costumes had been rented, true, but absolutely nothing fit! Evidently every soul in the cast had either lost weight, gained weight, grown taller, shrunk, or developed lumps where they hadn't had any before. I took in seams, let down hems, replaced zippers, glued headdresses back together, and worked for hours on five chiffon evening dresses that were made in the style of the twenties—tiers and tiers of ruffles, bows, rhinestone shoulder straps, and velvet trimming. The garments had evidently been made in the twenties, and worn often in the fifty years since then. The material was rotten and I had to mend those things every night for five weeks. I remember collapsing in exhausted hysterics against the strong manly shoulder of one of the actors after sewing a flounce on one dress for the fifth night in a row—and always during a five-minute break.

Anyway, I got the alterations done. Dorothy Lamour's shoes dyed to match her dresses, the blonde wigs for the dancers styled for the twenties (and re-styled because they were wrong,) and miles of sequins sewn onto four pair of angel wings. The dancers all had tap shoes that fit, and the taps had finally been put on so they suited everybody—after I'd had them done three times.

Cleaning is always a problem for a wardrobe mistress. Can it be washed? Can it be cleaned at all? Many of the costumes for *Anything Goes* were so old and rotten it was chancy, and when I sent anything to be cleaned I crossed my fingers.

It didn't work.

On opening night of the second week of the show one of the young female stars came running to me in a panic. Her second act costume had been cleaned on Monday, our one day off, and she hadn't tried it on until the first act break. It was form-fitting all right. She stood there, tears spotting a garment that had shrunk so badly that the poor girl's anatomy was completely obvious. My God! What to do. I had an extra white sailor suit like the boys were wearing. I quickly sewed the pants up so they had a lot more flair, cut off the sleeves of the jumper, added a flashy red tie and shoved her onstage.

The next day I had to find white crêpe and copy the original costume exactly. After all, it was rented and something had to be returned. I've often wondered if the rental company noticed that one costume was about thirty years newer than the others.

Dorothy Lamour will always be one of my favorite ladies. She is a "star". You feel it when you meet her, sensing it immediately when she walks on stage. She is a warm, friendly, sensitive woman.

A wardrobe mistress is usually a "dresser" for the star too, and, as a result, usually becomes better acquainted with her—or him, than the rest of the crew. Yes, I dress "hims" too. We have a small theater, and any boy employed there is needed to move scenery. Besides, I'm such a grandmotherly type that nobody objects. Actors seldom are bundles of modesty anyway. They can't afford to be, as quick changes must often be made in the wings. I wasn't Dorothy's dresser because I was needed downstairs. Many of the cast tended to panic if something ripped just before an entrance, and I'm an excellent zipper-fixer, safety-pinner, and shoulder-patter, so the theater hired dressers for Dorothy and Sterling (another dear person, even if I keep thinking of him as "Winnie the Pooh.") But more about that later.

Dorothy and I became friends anyway. She was sincerely interested in my children and grandchildren and how I made beef stew. A domestic lady herself, with a family of her own, also an affectionate person, we shared tears when the show was over, and she had to leave.

Jesse Peterson, the young male lead in the show, is probably best known for his part as Conrad Brodie in the movie, *Bye-Bye Birdie*. I really had expected a tall, good-looking, conceited ass, but was pleasantly surprised with a very tall, good looking, very nice young man.

In one scene Jesse was supposed to strip down to his underwear. One night, because of the quickness of the change, Jesse forgot to put on his shorts. He didn't realize it until he started to take off his trousers. I didn't see the scene but heard it downstairs. Every dressing room has a "squawk box" so the actors can hear their cues. (As a result, I can recite practically word for word about twenty-five shows just from hearing them eight times a week for four or five weeks.) Sterling realized that Jesse was shorts-less, and the resultant ad-libbing was a work of art. The audience never knew what had happened, but the cast and crew were practically helpless with laughter by the end of the scene.

Sterling Holloway is a small, wiry man with a cheerful

face and an explosion of pumpkin-colored hair. His voice is hard to describe, but its very uniqueness makes it perfect for Disney's cartoon characters. A fine actor, even Sterling can't remember how many movies he's been in, and he still keeps busy constantly.

Sterling needed a trick coat, shirt-front, and bowtie that could be changed quickly into a black-coat and white clerical collar—on stage. He also had to have his shoes fixed so one minute he had spats and the next minute none.

It took some trial and error on my part, but he was kind and helpful, and we succeeded. He could unsnap the bowtie, turn the collar around, tuck the fake spats into his shoes, and turn his coat inside out. It was reversible and, thank God, had been rented. Voilà—a clergymen instead of a gangster.

Of course, I won't pretend that every actor or actress is a delight to work with. There are quite a few I'd just as soon forget. Strangely enough though, it's very seldom the star who gives trouble. It's usually a bit player, who would like to be a star.

In *Anything Goes*, we had an aristocratic English lady who, although she was a good actress, was practically unknown. She was very sweet during the first rehearsals, but the test comes when the time gets short and pressure begins to build. Our lady began to find fault with things. Her shoes were too long, her dress was too short, the beads on the dress she had to wear kept dropping off. (It must've been a beautiful gown when originally made, but the years had taken their toll.)

Her part called for her to carry around a small dog all the time. She hated the dog and he felt the same about her. They had a scene together and every night she came offstage a little angrier. One night near the end of the run she stopped offstage with him under her arm. Before putting him down, she shook him and spanked his nose.

He promptly bit her on the thumb, and we nearly had a riot.

There are almost always problems when live animals are used in the show, but when there are temperamental actors, too, it can be awful.

I was kept busy during the show helping the actors with changes, mending old costumes that kept falling apart, cleaning spots off of white sailor outfits, and keeping peace among the inhabitants of the number two dressing room. All the girl dancers were crowded in with the girls from the chorus, and don't let anyone tell you there isn't a caste system in the theater.

There are constant squabbles. The dancers even fought among themselves.

"This is sure not mine," I heard one night as I walked past the dressing room. "I'm certainly not that fat."

"Well," came the answer, "at least my fat isn't all in my boobs."

I had to run in and stop it before they got to the hair pulling stage.

But that wasn't the worst. One night Dee Ann, one of the dancers, came running to me with a toe shoe in one hand and one of the satin ribbons in the other. She was furious.

"That bitch! She's so damn jealous because everybody watches me instead of her. Can you believe this? She cut the ribbon off my shoe," she sputtered.

Dee Ann had to be on stage right away so there wasn't time to do anything but use a safety pin and hope it would hold for the number.

Later when I had time to sew the ribbon back on, it was obvious that it really had been cut. There was never any proof as to who the culprit was, but Dee Ann was suspicious of one girl in particular, and the atmosphere in the dressing room grew more frigid each night.

Several of the boys were crowded into the tiny number four dressing room, and they, too, had problems. Since they all wore white sailor suits, they constantly got them mixed up. Red satin ties disappeared. Black socks evidently walked away. And tempers frayed.

Anything Goes was so successful it was held over for a week and played to full houses, but backstage everybody was getting touchy and we were all glad when closing night approached. There had been just too much "togetherness."

And I don't think I could have kept those chiffon dresses together one more night.

Broadway Zoo

During the three years I was a wardrobe mistress of the off-Broadway theater in San Diego, there were three shows that involved animals. Using animals on stage can cause real problems, especially if they haven't been specifically trained.

In *Anything Goes,* we worked with a small, mean Chihuahua. It had to be a small dog because one of our ladies had to carry it around all the time. Unfortunately, lady and dog hated each other. That got a bad start when, early in the run of the show, the actress got angry and spanked Woodie's nose, causing him to bite her thumb.

I had a problem with Woodie, too. On the day before dress rehearsal I was out in front, watching for costume problems, when the director yelled, "Trina." Directors never just talk—they whisper so you can't hear them, or holler so you wish that you couldn't.

"Trina, that dog needs a fur coat."

The Chihuahua didn't like the world or the show.

Now, I wasn't born yesterday. I'd heard about apprentices being sent for impossible, unheard of things, the left-handed monkey wrenches of the theater world. I laughed and said, "Sure, Mister Lucas, what color?"

"Brownish-red," he said "and you have to make a beard of the same fur that will hook over Jesse's ears."

My God, he was serious. I hadn't been told about the scene where the small, furry dog is led across stage, only to re-enter completely shorn. He is followed by Jesse, the young male lead, wearing a beard obviously made from the dog's coat.

I had two hours to find red-brown fur, make a coat for

the dog that could be ripped off in two seconds, and invent a beard with elastic that could hook over Jesse's ears.

I did it, but with no help from that nasty little animal. He disliked me from the beginning. He loathed me after he discovered that the coat rubbed against a very tender part of his anatomy. I remodeled it, but we never became friends.

In *Mister Roberts*, we had to use a live goat. Well, she was a gentle thing, but still smelled like a goat. Even though we kept her in the dressing room farthest from the others, it still wasn't pleasant. Harriet, our prop girl would "sit" with her during the show then take her home at night. The denizens of downtown Third Street got used to seeing a small girl and a white goat walking to Harriet's car late at night.

One night Pearl, the goat, got frightened on stage, and did what nervous animals do. The ship's captain didn't see the unpleasant mess and tracked it clear across stage. One of the sailors, in an effort to swallow his hysterics had a coughing fit. Another boy slapped him on the back and sprained his finger. Things went downhill after that, and it was a blessing the act was soon over.

Gypsy topped the "zoo bunch" with three animals. We needed a dog, a lamb, and a monkey. I didn't envy Harriet her job with that group.

To begin with, it was too late in the season to find a small lamb. The only one Harriet could find was practically a sheep and didn't want to perform. It hated show business, theater, prop friends, and people, in that order. Luckily, after three nights of unhappy bleating, the big lamb was sent home, and a toy was substituted.

We used three different poodles during the run of the show. The poor things got too nervous. Each of the dogs belonged to a crew member so Harriet only had to "dog-sit" during performances, but the dogs didn't get along with the monkey at all, and they had to be kept separated as much as possible.

The first monkey only lasted a week, then went home with whatever passes for a nervous breakdown in a monkey. The second one behaved all right on stage, but screamed fiercely when the crew was changing the scenery. In the original stage show, the monkey, a well-trained one, rode around on Mama Rose's shoulder. Herman, our monkey, wasn't trained. After two unfortunate accidents— one involving Kaye Ballard's hair— they decided to keep him in his cage and she carried him around.

Forty Carats

Pre-production week at the theater was known as "Hell Week."

"That's impossible."

"You're crazy—we've got at least fifteen minutes."

"God dammit, where's the fuckin' screwdriver?"

"These stupid damn screws ain't gonna fit in there anyhow. Hell, don't you know nothin'?"

"I could tell you what to screw."

"Hey, where's Tom?"

"Who the shit knows? Who needs him anyway? He don't know his ass from his elbow."

I grant you, it didn't sound like Mrs. Astor's afternoon tea and bridge party, but it did sound exactly like a tired, hard-working stage crew who'd been fighting against time—never enough time—to get an old show "struck" and a new one ready. We usually had only about twenty-four hours for a change-over, and it could get rough. Epithets flew, tempers exploded, and it was always perfectly obvious the show would never be ready.

It always was.

Somewhere there must be a friendly God who has a soft heart for show people, stage crews in particular.

At first, the crew's language shocked me, but after a couple of shows I came to realize that it was only a pressure escape valve and didn't mean much. I was the only female on the crew and, at first, the boys made a real effort to spare me some of the sounding off. Then along came Hell Week of *Forty Carats*. It was my third show.

There was a big cast for our very small theater and a lot of costume problems—some seemed insurmountable.

I had two impossible would-be stars to placate, and nothing was going right, I hadn't had any sleep for two nights and my sewing machine, a rented one with no policy, decided to die a shuddering death. I had begged for a new machine for weeks, and there I was with a stack of stuff to alter, an evening dress to build, and a dead sewing machine. I started up the stairs to find a shoulder to cry on and met the stage manager coming down.

"Hey, Trina", he said. I guess he was too tired to see the storm signals. "Would you sew up these drapes? The director wants them right away."

That did it. I remember charging up the stairs, stomping out onto the stage, (everybody, cast, crew, director, and producer where having a confab about something), and yelling, "Dammit, what do you want first, your costumes or your fuckin' curtains?"

Well, it was a silence so dead one would have thought the world had ended. And then, the laughter began. Trina wasn't a lady who swore, yet there was their sweet, pleasingly plump, prudish wardrobe mistress standing center stage, barefooted, hair flying, wearing dirty jeans and a baggy shirt with a torn sleeve. There she stood, swearing like a stagehand, yelling words she'd never used in her life. It must've been funny, and they never let me forget it. Still, I made my point. They bought me a new sewing machine the next day.

It was during Hell Week that I had my first run-in with the director. He'd been consistently nice to me up until then, but I knew he had a violent temper when pushed, and I avoided him whenever possible.

Well, the day before dress rehearsal I found out the male lead, Allen Hunt, needed a navy blue blazer. It had to be new, or almost, and had to really fit well. I didn't know where to borrow one as people didn't like to loan

19

good clothes to an actor. They're wicked. They use bad language. They're irresponsible. They wear make-up. They wear borrowed clothes to parties and spill liquor on them. These are not my words, but the beliefs of many theater-goers.

I think this is the right place to order a gold halo for man named Mr. Graph. He owned a fur store in town and loaned me gorgeous furs every time I needed one for show. He never charged me rent, but was happy with program credit and a couple of tickets to a performance. He trusted me to take care of $2,500 mink coats and I loved him. He was the kind of person who made a costumer's life a little easier.

But, back to my story. Jim, our stage manager, had forgotten to tell me about the coat. I knew how much he had to do, and I didn't blame him. That was the mistake that got me screamed at by the director. He caught me dead center stage, pinned me with the spotlight they were working on, and hollered,

"Where's the blue blazer, Trina?"

"I haven't been able to find one, yet."

"God dammit, what do you mean? We need it to rehearse with."

"I'm sorry, I didn't know he needed it. I was only told this morning." I was shaking.

"Jim should have told you. Where the hell's Jim?" He was hollering, now, and his face was turning red.

"Don't blame him. He's so busy he probably forgot."

"Jesus, God, and all the shitty angels. Don't tell me who to blame. That's the trouble with this damn theater. Everybody sticks up for everybody else. How the fuck can I find out what's going on when you all stick together like damn glue?"—This from the man who, when hiring me said, "I want us to be just one big happy theater family, all trusting one another."

20

I stood there like a criminal in a searchlight, praying I wouldn't cry. I cry when I get mad, when my feelings get hurt, or when I'm overly tired, and I was all three.

"Oh shit," he said, quieting down. I think he realized I was about to fall apart. "Go buy a damn blue blazer. It'll be hard enough to fit that skinny guy." (The director was built like a washtub.) Get the money from John."

I was off the hook. I ran downstairs, shut myself in the bathroom, and bawled. Later, when I told Jim I hoped I hadn't caused him any trouble, he just laughed, patted me on the shoulder and said, "Don't let old BB get to you. He barks worse than he bites."

I later learned BB stood for Baby Bastard.

Ed Binns was a favorite with the crew. Easygoing and soft spoken, he was pleasant to everyone. He and Marjorie Lord made a good pair. She wasn't temperamental, either, and, once *Forty Carats* got going, it ran smoothly.

Marjorie had eleven quick changes and Debby Rose, my assistant, dressed her while I busied myself with the other ladies who needed help, Audrey Christie, in particular.

Audrey's a fine actress, and a "character." She's loudly friendly, uninhibited, and never heard the word "modesty." Her dressing room door was always open, and backstage visitors were sometimes treated to the sight of a scantily dressed Audrey putting on her make-up

One of her costumes included a pair of bright red tights. One night I was downstairs sewing.

"Hey, Lovey, could you fix this dress for me?"

There stood Audrey, clad only in a bra and the red tights, and, with no offense intended, her figure was not great. A new, young male stagehand, whose shirt I'd been mending, turned scarlet, stuttered an incoherent greeting, and ran. Audrey wasn't embarrassed, but worried that he was upset.

"Poor thing," She said, patting her ample, red-clad stomach, "he's not used to all this middle-aged flab."

One day, during the run of *Forty Carats* an elderly lady friend asked me, "We saw your show Sunday. Tell me, why did those two young men with aerosol cans spray the stage during intermission?"

A strange question? A strange reason. Those two young men were stagehands and were trying vainly to get rid of gasoline fumes that were intoxicating the actors. A real motorcycle used in the first scene was left on stage each night, pre-set for the next performance. That Saturday night it had leaked gasoline and the next day no one knew why the actors came staggering off stage after each scene, gasping and silly. The play became more ragged as it progressed.

Finally, the first act was over and the source of the fumes discovered. No one knew what to do and the aerosol deodorant was tried as a last resort. It was a matinee performance and the audience of elderly people watched in bewilderment as the boys sprayed the stage, after first scrubbing it with soapy water. Nothing helped much and the play rambled on to its drunken conclusion. Luckily it was a comedy because it got funnier and funnier. Lines were lost and new ones invented on the spur of the moment.

Later, one of the backstage critics unkindly remarked that we should use gasoline more often—the play was more amusing that way.

Twenty Rutabagas

Toward the end of *Forty Carats*, we heard rumors about a party the cast was planning for the crew. There was always a cast party to which we were always invited, but never had there been one just to entertain us. Pretending we knew nothing about it, we decided to surprise them, too.

Many of our back-stage crew members were filling in time and gaining experience with hopes of someday being on the stage themselves. We had people painting backdrops, pounding nails and moving scenery who were more talented than some of the people in the shows.

Two of our talented crew members were conscripted to write a skit lampooning the show, called, naturally, *Twenty Rutabagas.* It was rehearsed in total secrecy and was ready in time for the party.

And what a marvelous party it was. Every cast member sang, did a monologue, played an instrument, or took part in a skit. We crew members acted surprised and delighted, which we were, then announced that we had a surprise for them, too. Our skit was wonderfully funny. We'd also discovered our young, quiet, bespectacled box office manager had a wonderful baritone voice, and one of our stagehands did a scene from *Beyond The Fringe*. I had even taught three of the stagehands a simple soft shoe dance that was fun. It was a great evening.

The Wimp

Wimpy, the head carpenter in our off-Broadway theater, had a perfectly ordinary name, William, but no one ever called him that. He'd worked in almost every theater in San Diego and for a long time in Las Vegas. He was known and respected for his technical knowledge, his dependability, and for a vocabulary far surpassing anything I'd ever heard. He was big, loud, belligerent, bossy, foul-mouthed, and, had the softest heart in the business.

When I was introduced to Wimpy he shook my hand, nearly mangling my fingers. "Well, goddamn— I worked with your dad. He was a great son-of-a-bitch. Glad to meet you. We *need* a lady around here—give this fuckin' place some class." Then, seeing something over my shoulder, he yelled, "My God! — don't you shit-asses know anything? Move that bloody thing sideways or you will screw up the whole fuckin' set."

Goodbye Apple-pie grandma, I thought. Hello theater world.

The wimp fought with everyone—except me. He yelled obscenities at everyone—except me. I soon learned to go to him for anything I needed—a table for my sewing machine, nails for pictures, a bulletin board, shelves for my thread and other paraphernalia, information about where to find almost anything to buy or borrow, help in moving things. He even saw to it that I had my own small toolset.

"And you shits keep your hands off her stuff, see? You can all do your screwin' with your own goddamned tools—"

By then, he saw us all laughing helplessly and realized what he'd said.

"Aw, hell," he said, "stop gargling like a pack of hyenas and get to work." But he laughed, too, and patted my shoulder before he stomped off

I soon learned that Wimpy had one vanity. He loved loud cowboy shirts. I had a piece of gaudy pink and purple fabric that I'd purchased for a show and never used.

Wimpy saw it one day and said wistfully, "Boy, wouldn't that make a bitchin' shirt? Like a cowboy shirt with all them little pearl buttons. Look— like this." He drew a surprisingly good sketch of a fancy shirt with a zigzagged cowboy yoke and sleeves with four button cuffs.

That night I swiped one of his work shirts out of the prop room so I could get his measurements, and two nights later was able to present him with a loud pink – purple shirt with "all the little pearl buttons," exactly like his sketch. I was amply rewarded when he just stood there looking at it before he spoke.

"Well goddamn—well Jesus Christ, goddamn." Then, being Wimpy, he said, "Too bad the pockets couldn't flap over more. Make it just about perfect." But I saw the wicked twinkle in his eye and knew he was thanking me.

The only times Wimpy ever got mad at me was when he thought I was being taken advantage of.

"You're being stupid," he'd say. "You're only one little ol' female." (He ignored the fact I was in no way *little*). "What do them bastards expect? Tell them to go screw themselves."

He knew, as I knew, I was the only "little old female" who could handle a needle, but he still yelled about it. And he didn't just yell. I found out after I got the new sewing machine, that Wimpy had created a real scene when he saw me cry that day. He was furious. "You'd better not risk losin' her," he told them. "She's the most important part of your crew," and insisted they get me the new machine.

Wimpy would never admit to a mistake, but depended on his loudness to get him out of anything. One night we were doing a show with Bob Crane that involved a bowling ball. It was Wimpy's job to get it out of the prop room and hand it to George, one of the stagehands. The Wimp tripped, dropping the ball down a whole flight of concrete stairs. I was on the other side of the stage, helping Bob with his costume change.

The scene on stage was a quiet one when suddenly we heard that thud— thud— thud—CRASH as the ball hit about every third step on the way down.

Bob had to make his entrance, not knowing what had happened, and when I got to the other side, Wimpy was just standing at the top of the stairs looking white. He had thought I was down by my ironing board, and he hadn't been able to shout a warning because of the scene on stage. The minute he saw that I was okay he turned on George and growled in a stage whisper,

"What the hell do you mean, missin' that ball when I handed it to you?" It was so typically Wimpy that we all laughed like idiots.

The Wimp moved to another job after I'd been there about a year and a half. The theater was a lot quieter, but he left a big void. Even though he constantly scolded and yelled at his "boys," he never allowed anyone else to treat them unfairly. They, and his "little old wardrobe female," thought the world of him.

V for Victory Canteen

The director of our new show, *Victory Canteen*, was giving me a list of clothes and accessories needed. Having gone through this many times before, I sat filling my notebook with exciting little items like black Spanish hats with red ball fringe, three cotton print sarongs,(for men, not for women.) Four "Carmen Miranda" outfits, complete with headdresses covered with plastic fruit. The list was long, and part of my mind was busy wondering where I'd find the things in only three days. Suddenly, the last thing he said penetrated my brain. A plaster cast for the male star's right arm—a removable cast he could slip on and off in seconds.

Well, I broke my arm about forty years ago, but didn't pay much attention to the method used to make the cast, being at the time in some pain, but George, one of the stagehands, offered to help. He worked as an orderly when in the Army. We bought a special kind of surgical gauze and made a sloppy mess in the bathroom because the stuff had to be soaked before using. We dripped wet plaster on the floor, on the wash basin, on George, on me, and everything else in the vicinity.

We finally got the wet cast on my arm. I had to continue working while it dried. Of course, it was on my right arm and I'm totally right-handed. The cast was heavy and got warmer and warmer as it dried – really uncomfortable.

It was finally dry enough to take off. George had carefully padded it with newspaper so there was extra room inside, but he had shaped it around my elbow and it wouldn't slip off. Panic! I visualized the wardrobe mistress spending the rest of the day with a heavy cast on her only intelligent arm.

George finally went to the surgical supply store and bought a pair of crooked scissors so he could carefully clip the upper part of the cast. I painfully slipped my arm out and we patched the seam with plaster. Did I volunteer to hold it while it dried? No sir.

Unfortunately for the theater costumer, many of our best actors and actresses are either gigantic or tiny. It's great for the producer to be able to find a six foot giant, an old midget, or a funny fat lady when he needs one, but they create headaches for the wardrobe mistress.

Marvin Miller was in our show. He is best remembered for his role in *The Millionaire*, a radio and television show produced some time ago. He has a deep, resonant speaking voice and is much in demand for narration, especially poetry, which he also writes beautifully.

But Marvin had gained a lot of weight. I was embarrassed when my tape measure wouldn't go around him, but he laughed.

"Kinda fat, huh? Here, I'll hold the end so you can get the rest of the way around."

I was relieved he had a sense of humor about his weight. Lots of people don't, and it takes diplomacy when making and fitting costumes for them.

I didn't have any trouble finding trousers and shirts at our local large men's store, but the script also called for a World War I Army jacket and Marvin had to sing while wearing it so it couldn't be too tight.

Well, there aren't many clothes left from that period, and certainly none as large as we needed. I called every costume rental agency, the Army, even a friend's grandfather who knew someone who knew someone else.

No luck.

There wasn't time to build a coat and I was about ready to admit defeat. But a costumer can't give up. The day of dress rehearsal I rented the largest Army coat I could find of that period. I let out the seams as much as possible and told Marvin I thought the whole thing would be funnier if his coat wouldn't button. After all, it was supposed to be 1944 and the character would have certainly put on some weight. He agreed, the director agreed, and I was off the hook.

Patty Andrews, of the beloved Andrew Sisters, was our Lady Star, and a lovely one. She got along with everyone and was never temperamental. The only Andrews sister still performing, her voice was still wonderful.

I can't say the same for our young male lead. The voice was okay, but not the disposition. He fussed and fumed because his scarf wouldn't "flip" right in one of his scenes. I tried three different scarves, (it had to be silky and it had to be white,) finally sewed a nickel in each end of the one I'd made originally. It worked and I kept mum about the whole thing.

There was always a party on opening night after the show. They were gala affairs with plenty of liquor and tables loaded with an abundance of beautiful hors d'oeuvres and canapés. These parties were held so the cast and press could charm each other, but we were all invited. While there, we were introduced to the stars who had come down from Hollywood to see the show. During the three years I worked at the theater I met many actors I'd seen in the movies and on TV. Jane Wyman, Martha Raye, Paul Lynde, Richard Deacon, Andy Griffith, Steve Allen, Jane Meadows, Zsa Zsa Gabor, and Jack Klugman, to name a few.

Of course everyone dressed "to the teeth." Crew members who had spent weeks in their grubbies backstage, blossomed out in gorgeous plumage on opening night. We hardly recognized each other.

Victory Canteen was a difficult show to costume. Musicals are always more complicated to dress than straight plays. We received the costumes from the original show, but they were in such bad condition that few of them could be used. Evidently someone had swept up the floors of the Los Angeles theater dressing room and simply dumped everything in cardboard boxes. We never did find out what some of the stuff were – maybe things from another show.

By opening night I was exhausted. Everything was done, but had been only finished shortly before curtain time. I had brought fabric to make myself a new long dress for the party but hadn't had time to even cut it out.

I looked down at what I was wearing. My God. Faded stretch pants, (stretched to the limit,) a baggy shirt with half the shirttail missing, (one of the dancers had needed a quick bandage job during rehearsal.) I had on a bra that allowed me to sag comfortably, and no shoes. I never wore shoes when I worked and had no idea where they were. Luckily my hair was clean and short so it only needed brushing. There was a pair of hose and some earrings in my emergency kit. I never knew when I might have to look human.

I looked at the pieces of fabric with the pattern pinned to them. I felt like I'd been sewing for days. I had. But if I wanted to go to the party I had no alternative.

"Look, kids," I told the dancers, "I'm going to try to make my dress between now and curtain call. If you tear anything, pin it. It'll never show from the front. In a dire emergency, I'll be here, but please don't bother me unless it's really drastic."

Bless them all. They spread the word and I was left strictly alone with my sewing machine. Every once in a while someone would creep down to the ironing board to press something, whisper, "How's it going?" and silently disappear again.

I finished the dress as the applause died down at the end of the show. I found my shoes behind the water heater and had purposely made the dress long enough so no one would see them. Black sneakers aren't considered stylish with an evening gown.

Barefoot and Comfortable

Returning to the theater after a short vacation, I found them preparing for *Barefoot in the Park*, starring Tab Hunter.

Tab Hunter

My assistant had begun to shop for necessary clothes and, as she turned the job back to me, vowed darkly, "You'll hate him. He's impossible to please."

I liked Tab. He was particular, yes, but actually that made my job easier. He had done the role before and knew exactly what he needed to wear. The hardest thing to find was a dark gray "Chesterfield," the type of overcoat seldom worn in California. Luckily, it was late summer and thrift shops were selling heavy coats for practically nothing. Instead of running back and forth exchanging things, I simply bought four gray overcoats— can you imagine, at ten cents each?— and showed them to Tab. He pounced on one, pronounced it "perfect," and we were friends. I put the others in our wardroom to use in later shows.

Tab was generous with his appreciation, never taking it for granted, as many actors did, that a garment had simply dropped from heaven when I snapped my fingers. He was a comfortable star to work with. He wore old jeans, was friendly without being condescending, and talked about his horses and dogs instead of show business. And he didn't stare at himself in the mirror while talking to me. This happens often with actors, and is disconcerting.

I like to remember *Barefoot*. Seldom does a show continue smoothly backstage for four whole weeks. Personalities clash, tempers are lost, and sometimes people just get bored with the show. *Barefoot in the Park* was one of the unusual ones. Everyone liked everyone else, and we were plagued with very few problems.

Dressing room number two, our biggest room downstairs, was a favorite hangout. Because the cast was small, the room was shared by only two men, Jerry Nawrocky and Frank La Verdi, both fine character actors. They delighted in cheerfully insulting each other. Any of us who weren't busy sat in their dressing room, played word games, and helped Jerry and Frank think up insults.

Every night when one of them came downstairs after a scene, the other would be ready with some monstrous put-down.

"Hey," said Frank one night, "there's a good lookin' broad in the second row that's got the hots for me."

"Yeah," drawled Jerry, I saw her, too. She wouldn't be bad without the white hair, cane, and two hearing aids. The black wart on her chin was kind of a turn-off, though."

Or—

Jerry: "Watch it, they're real vicious tonight. They'll probably like you, though. They're all little old ladies from Pasadena."

One night Jerry's toolbox, (he was playing a telephone repair man,) fell open and his tools fell all over the stage.

"Shit," isn't the most original ad-lib in the world, but the audience loved it. Jerry was upset, though, and came stomping downstairs convinced that the scene had been ruined. As he stormed into the dressing room, I hopefully awaited Frank's hazing.

He tried, he really did, but all he could do was stand there, waving his hands and laughing helplessly.

Soon Jerry was laughing, too.

Frank finally did manage a weak smile. "Some bastards'll do anything to steal a scene."

"Ha," exclaimed Jerry. "Didja hear that audience? They know who the real star of the show is."

"Get away from the sink," Frank said to me, "I think I'm going to throw up."

In one of Frank's scenes he was supposed to hobble around on an injured foot. There wasn't time between scenes to get a real bandage on and off, so we put three heavy gym socks on the floor each night.

One evening Jerry was teasing Frank, as usual. "Hey, Frank, put on your human face, now. It's almost time for your big entrance. Mustn't scare any babies." Then as Frank started up the stairs, "Hey, you bandaged the wrong foot."

Frank nearly missed his entrance.

Another night when dressing to go home, Jerry said, "How'd ya like my new sweater?" He should've known better than to ask.

Frank's answer, "How'd ya get the dog to give it up?"

Jerry got even.

The next night Frank choked on a piece of meat he was supposed to be eating, forgot his lines, and caused Tab to quickly add-lib. Then Frank finished the ragged scene by bringing his cane down smartly on his own instep. Hobbling painfully, he bravely waited to yell until he got downstairs.

Jerry was ready for him. In total silence he guided Frank to a chair, tore up an old T-shirt, and carefully proceeded to apply a bandage, not to Frank's foot, but to his mouth.

Plaza Not So Sweet

When I found out the costumes for the second show, *Plaza Suite* would not be rented, I got scared again.

"They'll furnish most of their own clothes," the director said. "You only have to shop for a few things."

Well that didn't sound too awful. Not until I found out what the "few things" were.

Dana Andrews needed a complete set of tails. So did Michael Phillips, who worked in the box office and had a small part in the show. That shouldn't be much trouble. There was a tuxedo shop in town that rented dress clothes.

Then....

"Remember, Dana's coat has to be ripped up the back every night on stage, then soaked in water for the storm scene later."

Whoopee! Well, I was new at the wardrobe game, but no one else knew any more than I did, so it was up to me to cope. I ended up renting two tail coats, ripping one very carefully at the back and sewing Velcro on both sides of the raw seams.

Velcro is a costumer's savior, used anytime garments had to be removed or put on quickly. It also makes a lovely ripping sound when used on stage. The coat trick was a resounding success. The other coat got soaked in a bucket of water every night for the storm scene. My biggest problem was getting it dried and put back together between shows on matinee days. That was solved using a hair dryer belonging to one of the actresses.

I was proud of my ingenuity and waited to be

complimented. Nothing was said, and I learned right away that all that wonderful "talent" of mine was evidently taken for granted. I eventually learned to take that as a compliment, but it took a while.

Mike Biers and Candy Chapell, theater employees, had small parts in the show. All Mike had to have was a waiter's jacket, but Candy needed a wedding gown. The jacket I was able to borrow from a nearby hotel, and I was in luck because Candy had been married recently, and I rented her gown for a small fee.

I began to breathe easier. Then they dropped the bellboy bomb. The director was determined that the bellboy in the play be dressed in a navy blue jacket with gold buttons. I couldn't find one to rent, or buy, so I offered to make it, or in theater language, "build" it. He looked amazed and said,

"Could you?" I didn't know then that many wardrobe mistresses can't really sew well. Your job is to take care of rented or borrowed clothes, see that they're cleaned and mended, sometimes replacing a button or zipper.

I assured him I was capable of building a bellboy's jacket and immediately found out what happens to people who volunteer.

"Would you make three?" he asked. "I think it would look great if the boys who change the sets between acts would wear them, too."

We weren't using a curtain so the audience could see the changes being made.

Well, I brought it on myself. I built three.

Pam Britton was our Lady Star in *Plaza Suite*. She played three completely different characters, so had to be outfitted accordingly. I wasn't happy when the director told me to take her shopping with me. I had already learned that most actors have very definite ideas about their costumes. The main one is to look thin, thin, thin.

One of the ladies who Pam was portraying was supposed to be rather dowdy, and a little overweight.

Oh, God, I prayed. *How will I talk her into it?* She had a slim, beautiful figure and looked about twenty-five years old.

I shouldn't have worried. Pam was an actress. She had studied each of the three characters carefully and knew exactly what each should wear. We agreed on everything, had a lovely lunch, compared pictures of our children and were friends from then on.

Pam needed a "mother of the bride" hat for the third act. We found the perfect dress, but it was aqua crepe and the only bridal hats were white.

I did it again.

"Why don't I get some aqua colored lace and cover it?" I asked.

Dana Andrews and I got off to a rather poor start. He didn't like the way I ironed his shirts. They were his own shirts, beautifully custom-made, but made of fabric my iron just laughed at. I didn't really blame him for being upset. I don't iron well, probably because I hate the job. If I had my way the creator of permanent-press would have stars in his crown.

Anyway, Dana got cross and "God damned" my ironing, I got my feelings hurt and sulked behind the water heater. I later learned that Dana "God damned" everything and that it didn't mean much, but, at the time I thought he hated me.

He wanted his trousers taken in.

I should have talked him out of that. They were too big, and with the amount of sitting he had to do in the show, he needed room in the seat. However, he was a "star" and I, a lowly wardrobe person.

I made his trousers smaller, then sat through dress rehearsal in the darkened theater, dying, as I realized the back seam of his pants split the first time he sat down. There was nothing I could do. He didn't come offstage until the end of the first act. I just sat, imagining, with hot flashes and cold chills, what he was going to say to me.

What did he say?

"Sorry, I guess I put on a little weight. When you sew them up, maybe they shouldn't be quite so tight."

I was able to breathe again.

And, would you believe he asked me to make him some new shirts, (of a different material,) because I sewed so beautifully. Neither of us even mentioned ironing again.

Summer Storm with Grasshoppers

As a theater wardrobe mistress, I had one recurring nightmare. It was show-time and I had forgotten to pick up costumes from the cleaners.

One night it happened.

We were doing *Storm in Summer*, a Rod Serling play that was having its first try-out in our theater. We had a good cast, including Sam Jaffe, Patty McCormack, and Edd Byrnes, well known from the TV series *77 Sunset Strip*. It hadn't been a difficult show to costume because the actors wore their own clothes. I only had to furnish a few odds and ends.

Edd had four changes during the play, and after dress rehearsal I took his shirts to be cleaned for opening night.

Sam Jaffe

When I went to pick them up they weren't finished, and they asked me to come back later. Having a slight headache, I drove home, took a couple of aspirins, put my feet up and relaxed.

I woke at 6:15. The cleaners closed at 6:00. Oh, God, my nightmare had happened for real. What to do? Well, the stores were still open and I had until 7:00 to buy four shirts. Calling Edd was one of the most difficult things I've ever had to do. He hadn't been a very pleasant person to work with, and I had to tell him I didn't have his shirts for opening night.

He wasn't a bit happy, but evidently realized how miserable I felt because he didn't yell at me. I told him I was going shopping and checked with him on sizes and styles.

"I'd really like a dark red velour with long sleeves", he told me. "And one of those golf shirts, blue, with a penguin on the pocket". The velour would be all wrong for the play, but he was being so nice I told him I'd try to find one.

Well, it was the day after Christmas. All the stores were having sales. There were dozens of bargain hunters in every store, and not nearly enough salespeople. I only had an hour to try to find a medium-sized red velour shirt with long sleeves, but I did. It was pure luck, and expensive, but Edd had wanted it so badly I hoped he'd buy it after the show.

Edd Byrnes

But there weren't any blue golf shirts at all. I finally got a salesgirl's attention, then asked about golf shirts.

"I'll look, if you want me to," she said, but didn't move.

"Please?" I asked.

She meandered over to another counter, stopping to speak to a young man on the way, not business, but just "Hi, there," with an "I'm available" smile.

She eventually returned, in no perceptible hurry, with a pile of shirts. There were no blue shirts, no golf shirts, no penguins, and, finally, no medium shirts.

I gave up. I grabbed three other shirts that I thought would be suitable, and broke every speed record getting to the theater.

Edd met me at the stage door. "I found some shirts I can use", he said. (I kept my ugly thoughts to myself). He did like the red velour shirt, though, and wore it that night – and only that night. I was able to take the other shirts back, but had to pay for the red one. At least my husband really liked it. I never told him how much it cost.

Everyone expects ex-child stars to be difficult to work with. Not so. Angela Cartwright, from the *Danny Thomas Show*, and Brandon deWilde, who had been in the movie, *Shane*, had both worked in our theater. They were both quiet, professional, and easy to work with. Patty McCormack was in *Storm in Summer*, and was one of the sweetest people I've ever known. She was also an excellent actress.

Patty McCormack

Another fallacy is that all child actors are undisciplined monsters. We used four small boys in *Gypsy* and had more trouble with the adults than with the youngsters. Danny Wyngard, age 10, was in *Under Papa's Picture* and spent all his spare time reading and doing crossword puzzles in the dressing room.

Twelve-year-old Rodney was in *Storm in Summer*. Handsome, mahogany-colored, with a neat halo of black frizz, he was a charmer. He had an amazing vocabulary and used it to such an extent that it was only necessary for us to grunt a monosyllable once in a while to keep the conversation going.

One night between acts he told me the whole plot of the movie he'd seen on TV.

"You see, there are big giant grasshoppers, and they's eatin' up Chicago. Boy, how ugly. And I know why there were so many, I bet it was their matin' season. That's why they all came to one place, I bet." His brown eyes were shining.

You never knew where his conversation would lead next. But he was a good actor, and never missed the cue.

"You see this, ma'am?" Rodney held up a wire cake cutter.

"What's that for? I asked.

"Well, for you it'd cut up an angel cake, but it's my comb." He demonstrated, then smiled at me and said, "I'd loan it to you but y'all got the wrong kind of hair. It's gotta be like curly wool."

I found myself wishing all I had to do with my mouse-colored hair was comb it with an angel-food cake-cutter. It would sure save trips to the beauty shop.

On opening night, I met Rod's mother and complimented her on her son's behavior. I admired her even more later. I had just helped Rod get ready for the first act and watched him trot up the stairs. Just as I was turning back, I saw him running down again—in a completely different outfit. I couldn't believe what I was seeing.

"Rod?" I asked.

"No ma'am, I'm Ron." They were identical twins, and both in show business. I'll bet Mom had her hands full when both live-wires were at home.

The show went well after the opening night problems. I never got to like Edd very well, but the rest of the cast was friendly and fun—and Don, my husband, loved his red velour shirt.

Hey, Mr. Roberts, Your Mistress Dyed!

Every time we planned a show that had a soldier, sailor, marine, WAAC, WAAF, or even a policeman in the cast, I suffered.

This meant there would be uniforms with a hundred kinds of stripes, pins, sleeve and hat insignias, all of which must be *right*. The problem was that no two people ever agreed on what was *right* especially if it was a period show.

Any show depicting a different time rather than contemporary is considered "period." The twenties and thirties are used often, and the turn of the century is also popular with the playwrights. This type of show is always a headache for the costumer unless she has a lot of time and a budget big enough to allow everything to be designed and built. It can be exciting when you're able to start from scratch and have everything coordinate, but a small theater can't afford that luxury. The costumer has to try to find things in thrift shops, old clothing stores, and friends' attics, or trade favors with other theater costumers by borrowing or renting.

A period military costume seems to be anything that was used prior to the day-before-yesterday. The Army, Navy, and Marines change their minds about uniforms more often than women change hair styles. The locale of the play also makes a difference. The marines on an island in the Pacific didn't wear anything similar to the ones in New York City even if it was the same year. There is a proper uniform for the tropics at tea time, Alaska in the spring, a ditch in France, a cocktail party in Zanzibar, or an air battle over Panama. Not to mention morning, afternoon, or evening, summer, winter, spring, fall, or the Queen's Coronation (any queen). Each occasion seems to have required a different uniform, and I haven't yet discovered a way to be sure I'm correct. The old ex-admiral who kept the Navy "on its toes" in 1930 will violently disagree with the old ex-admiral who was on the ship next door as to what was worn. Research books are just as bad. No two agree on how the insignias were properly worn.

Thank God I'm not young, blonde, and beautiful. I've been known to stop uniformed men in the street to ask questions about their clothes. In our part of town especially, my motives could be misconstrued.

I may have become overly sensitive about it all, but it seems as if about eight out of ten playwrights stick a uniformed man (or a dozen) in their plays just to exasperate me. In my first show, *Anything Goes*, circa 1930, the whole male dance chorus was sailors. In *Everybody's Uniform*, a Korean War period, there were four sailors. In *Victory Canteen*, 1944, a soldier, sailor, marine, and an old World War I veteran (who had to have a uniform coat) In *Lenny*, I had to outfit a Hitler and an Eichmann, and I'm convinced that every time a playwright needed a part for his brother-in-law, he added a policeman to his play. Their uniforms are different in every town and county as well.

The final blow to my morale came when the management decided to produce *Mister Roberts*. Seventeen actors had to be outfitted in the uniforms of a 1945 Navy. There were enlisted men, a captain, a couple of lieutenants, a boatswain's mate, a WRAC nurse, a ship's doctor, an MP, an SP, the list seemed endless. To make matters stickier, even though the producer had taken pity on me and hired a military expert as technical advisor, there were eight men in the cast who had been in the service at about that time, and no two of them agreed with the expert on anything. Our theater business manager had been in the Navy himself during that period and remembered things in such a positive manner that I listened to him. Wrong! He was incorrect about a dozen things, as was our military consultant. I talked to people at the Navy Recruiting Office, the Naval Training Center, the library, the bar next door (always full of ex-military personnel trading tall stories), the locker clubs (usually run by old ex-sailors) and a fascinating vintage sea captain who lived on a decrepit houseboat and remembered things differently after each drink.

I shopped for days to find uniforms that could be used, and I changed sleeve insignias so often I nearly wore out the fabric.

One of the costume problems in *Mister Roberts* was that except for officers, the men had to look like they'd been at sea for months. This made it necessary to "age" their work uniforms. I managed to find some old dungaree pants and chambray shirts, but the rest I had to buy new and try to make them look like the old ones. No real trouble, just stick them in a bathtub of diluted bleach—except that I didn't have time to go home, even to sleep, for three days before the show. And home is where I keep my bathtub. Finally, at 2:00 A.M. dress rehearsal morning, I drove home, filled the tub with water, bleach, and twelve pairs of dungarees. It worked beautifully. After they dried, they looked old and faded, so in with the shirts. That was a mistake. Fourteen shirts instantly turned a horrid muddy gray, not streaked or even faded-looking, just gray (not a naval color even after months at se.) I sat down and looked at those damned useless things and wept. Then I washed my face, drove to an all-night market, bought some blue dye, and dyed all those shirts again, stirring them only slightly so they'd streak. It worked, but I had to beg the laundry to always wash them in cold water so the dye wouldn't come out and leave them gray again.

Opening night was behind us. After two frantic weeks of rehearsing, painting sets, recording music and sound effects, and aging dungarees, *Mister Roberts* opened successfully. Fifteen men of assorted sizes, shapes, and temperament were costumed. The revolving stage with its three sets turned quickly and quietly, and after the opening night excitement of flowers, champagne, and celebration, we relaxed.

We shouldn't have.

Anyone connected with show business dreads the second night of a play. There's always a let-down from the electrical excitement of opening night and everyone has to work extra hard not to transmit that feeling to the audience.

The second performance of *Mister Roberts* was unbelievable! My first inkling that all was not well was the appearance in my wardrobe room of a young man I'd never seen before. He said he needed a costume because he was taking Tom's place. Tom was one of the two stagehands who doubled as a sailor in the show. Upon questioning the new boy, I learned that Tom and Gary, the other stagehand, were in jail and no one knew why or for how long.

I was able to costume the boy, and he was quickly coached in his stage actions. The big problem, however, was the fact that our two jailbirds were the only people who knew how and when to rotate the stage. Fred, the doorman, was conscripted to take Gary's place, but it was show time and no one had a chance to tell the new hands what to do.

It was disastrous. Everyone was so nervous and so helpful that the stage rotated once when it wasn't supposed to, almost upsetting James Drury, who was playing the title role. The second scene was played on half of a stage because it hadn't been turned far enough. Once it turned so slowly that the lights came on, catching the makeshift crew pushing, shoving, and using some extremely salty language.

To make matter worse, Pearl, the ship's mascot, a gentle white goat we had borrowed, became nervous and did what all nervous animals do—on stage! The ship's captain didn't see the unpleasant mess and tracked it clear across the stage. One of the sailors, in an effort to swallow his hysterics, nearly strangled and had a coughing fit. Another boy slapped him on the back and sprained his finger.

As we rapidly went from bad to worse, Kevin O'Neal, who played the role of Ensign Pulver, got a mouthful of soapsuds in a scene where he is splashed with soapy water. He stood gasping and couldn't say his lines until "Mister Roberts" intelligently handed him a glass of colored water that was supposed, to be strong homemade whiskey. The audience must have been mystified when the ensign took a large swallow of raw whiskey to stop coughing.

Drew Handley, the sound technician, wasn't immune, either. When Mister Roberts throws the captain's beloved potted palm overboard, he used a marvelous recorded splash. On that unforgettable night, Drew turned the tape on late. When the splash finally came, it sounded as if the ship was a hundred feet out of the water.

The final straw occurred during the curtain calls. When James Drury stepped forward for his bow, all the lights went out and stayed out. Jim was unhappy about that, and not quietly. By that time, all of us backstage were so demoralized that we were limply hysterical and talking seriously about leaving show business forever.

Luckily, after that night, everything went smoothly, but it would be a long time before we'd allow ourselves to get complacent again.

Drew, Shirley, and Fred

Drew Handley and his wife, Shirley, were part of our theater family. Drew could do anything. He was an actor, and a good one, had directed, produced, worked on scenery, lights, sound—anything connected with the theater, he'd done. He was an affable, patient man who rarely lost his temper or raised his voice. A handsome, white-haired Texan, he was often given parts in our plays.

Shirley was a voice teacher and actress. She taught in Los Angeles and would come to San Diego every weekend to be with Drew. She was small and blonde, and always willing to listen sympathetically to anyone's problems. Drew and Shirley hadn't been married very long (it was a second marriage for each) and they adored each other.

The three of us became good friends, having two loves in common: show business and food! They both loved to eat, and one has only to look at me to know it's a hobby of mine as well.

Drew was given a speaking role in *Forty Carats*, and had a line that caused the longest laugh of any show we did. He played the part of a gentlemanly Texas millionaire with a rich drawl, and in one scene asked Marjorie Lord to decorate his apartment.

"With, you know, curtains and drapes and all that shit."

Well, he always threw the last part of the line away, which means not putting any emphasis on it, and the laugh was slow in starting. Then, when the audience realized what he'd said, and how incongruous it was for the character he was portraying, the laugh would grow and grow. We used to count the seconds backstage each night and make bets on how long it would stretch out.

Drew and Shirley both had roles in *Guys and Dolls,* and they were good, but my favorite of Drew's parts was a walk-on in *Barefoot in the Park.* He portrayed a delivery man who had just struggled up six flights of stairs carrying a lot of packages. Ile didn't say anything, just pantomimed his part. He nearly stole the show every night. His gasping and facial expressions were so funny that the audience always applauded him as he made his exit. It was proof of what a good actor could do with a small part. I seldom saw much of any play from the front since I was usually dressing someone, and frankly, unless it was something really special, hearing the show eight times a week was enough. Drew was something special. Every night I would sneak out through the side door in the dark to watch his performance.

Fred Hayden was another good friend. I hesitate to name him "janitor" or "doorman." because, although he was both, he did so many other things in our theater that those two names don't suffice.

Fred was a tall, dignified black man with a rollicking sense of humor and a love of snappy clothes and cast parties. He lived at the theater, literally. 'There was a small storage space under the stage where he had his bed, and he usually kept his clothes and razor in dressing room number four. Evidently the ghost never bothered him.

Fred was willing to help with anything. When we were building a new show, he'd work on the lights and help with the sets, as well as perform his regular janitorial duties. The whole theater was carpeted, with the exception of the stage, so he had to vacuum constantly. There were five bathrooms and seven dressing rooms to keep clean, and it was also his job to order the supplies we needed. Fred would work all day, helping everyone, then quickly clean up and change into his black trousers and red and gold doorman's coat. Then he'd stand in front of the theater and help the ladies out of their cars, hold doors, greet people, and answer questions.

Fred knew everything about the theater, the play, the actors, and the crew. Or, if he didn't know, he could make anyone believe he did. He loved to talk and was always telling me who was being paid how much, who was having trouble with the wife or girl friend, what problems the management was having with the star, and what he, Fred, could do to improve things around there.

Unhappily, he also told everyone how to do his or her job better, and that kind of help wasn't always appreciated.

Cactus Flower And A Few Thorns

Many shows have some costume changes that have to be accomplished so quickly the actor must change in the wings. I've already said that I worked not only as wardrobe mistress, but also as a dresser, sometimes for one actor or actress, but often for everyone in the show who needed help. Once in a while things got a little frantic.

During *Cactus Flower* I had only two people to dress, but it might as well have been ten. There were fourteen "black-out" changes for Virginia Mayo and Tod Andrews. This meant there were only seconds between the time the lights went out for one scene and on again for the next.

Virginia Mayo

Tod's changes weren't too difficult except that they were fast, and he was nervous, but Virginia's entailed a complete change of outfit every time—dress, shoes, bag, even jewelry. For two scenes she also had to change her hair style in just minutes. Thank heaven for wigs and hair pieces. They're a God-send in the theater. It's the dresser's job to be sure each costume has been "preset," or placed, where the actor changes. The clothes must be in exactly the same place and in the same order for each performance. Quick changes are choreographed almost like a dance—first down with the zipper, then off with the dress, on with the slacks and shirt, the actress zipped and buttoned by the dresser, shoes stepped into by the actress, belt buckled by dresser, hair parted by actress, bag handed by dresser, and off goes actress while dresser breathes with relief. One more quick change accomplished.

Luckily, Virginia was a real pro. She seldom got nervous, and we were able to plan her changes together so even the seemingly impossible ones were working by opening night.

The sets for *Cactus Flower* were on a turntable. This made it possible to have three sets on the stage at one time and the stagehands merely revolved the stage during the blackouts. I had to learn exactly when and where Virginia and Tod would be exiting, and be there with a flashlight and, in Tod's case, a good steady hand grip.

Poor Tod went completely blind and panicked every time the lights went out. I learned to always be where I could reach out and grab him immediately. He was one of those unfortunate actors whose eyes never adjusted to a blackout, and he had to be led off stage, helped with his change, and led back on again.

Tod died in 1972, and we all felt a sense of loss. He was so nice to work with, so unfailingly courteous to everyone. I'm glad to remember that he learned to trust me completely, and I never let him down by not being there with a helping hand.

The *Cactus Flower* sets were awful. The theater management, to save money probably, had ordered them from Los Angeles instead of having our boys build them at the theater.

As a result of poor planning and designing, the sets arrived unfinished, undecorated, and didn't fit the stage. There were such big spaces left unmasked (any opening that allows the audience to see backstage is usually "masked" by a flat or a curtain) that the audience saw more of me running around behind the scenes than they did the play. One newspaper critic was unkindly truthful enough to say that the set depicting the dentist's office looked like "a deserted bus station at 3:00 A.M." The whole thing was so badly constructed that bookcases broke and pictures hung crookedly. One night a door stuck and Tod had to yell the first half of one of his scenes from behind it. Another night, in a scene where he had to angrily slam that same door, the whole side of the wall collapsed, luckily hurting no one, but giving the audience an excellent view of backstage and scurrying stagehands.

Virginia was hard to get acquainted with. She was a quiet, reserved lady and didn't seem to trust me at first. After the show got going, however, she warmed up and we got along well. She wore her own clothes, beautiful ones, and the only thing I had to get for her was a nurse's uniform.

Virginia's uniform wasn't hard to find, but Tod needed a dentist's coat that could be put on and taken off in seconds—in the dark. Dear old Velcro again. What would I have done without it?

It's a wonder I didn't get thin during *Cactus Flower*; I spent the whole evening, every evening, running back and forth between Virginia and Tod. Some of the costume changes took place in their dressing rooms, but most of them were in the wings, or even on stage. And nearly always in the dark.

Tod had one really tough change. As the lights went out and the stage began to revolve, I had to get him off the turntable, get his clothes changed, be sure he had a pencil, hand him a coat box, see that he was in the right place for the next scene, and, using ear phones, let the stage manager know we were ready. One night I got tangled up in the ear phone cord, fell off the turntable, and pulled poor Tod down with me. We didn't break anything or anyone, but the next scene was a little late getting started.

Cactus Flower offered the stage crew one nice thing. One of the three sets had an oversized bed. It wasn't particularly comfortable, having been built of wood and covered with a thin layer of form rubber, but it was big and had pillows. Although the set was only used twice in the show, the bed was in constant use. It was a busy show for the whole crew, with lots of sets, props, and costume changes, and although there were rules about drinking and smoking backstage, no one had ever said anything about lying down. Anyone who wasn't busy during a scene relaxed, and there were sometimes five people on that bed at one time. On matinee days it was used for naps between shows by whoever got there first. I was considered one of them now and got my nap only if I was one of the first three to get there. We allowed five for "resting," but only three for serious napping. My sense of humor is such that I went home after our first long "two-show" day and told my husband I had slept with two stagehands between shows. I was a little deflated when he said, straight faced, "Good— I'm glad you got some rest."

Starring Eve Arden and Trina Grieg

Brooks West

My acting debut at the off-Broadway theater was a walk-on part in *Under Papa's Picture*, starring Eve Arden and her husband, Brooks West. Nearly everyone on the crew had been drafted for walk-on duty at one time or another, but I always insisted I was too busy.

This time I was talked into it. I was there. I was the right size, age, and color. And, they wouldn't have to pay me, (a good reason for using crew walk-ons.) The stage-struck kids who worked backstage were so delighted to appear with the star that they'd do it for nothing. I guess the management figured me for a stage struck middle-aged woman. I agreed, not because I was anxious to be on stage again, but because the manager gave me such a heartrending sob story. I would be so good. There wasn't anyone else, etc. etc. etc.

It was a nuisance. Eve had six costume changes, and I had to run downstairs right after her fifth change and quickly get out of my working grubbies and into a girdle, hose, dress, coat, hat, gloves, pearls, high-heeled shoes, and makeup. I then had to scurry back upstairs for my entrance. Poor George Boyd, our nervous stage manager, never got used to me skidding into position at the last minute, but I always made it.

I'll have to admit, after I got the change smoothed out,

it was fun. All I had to do was make an entrance, register shock at the sight of an obviously pregnant woman getting married, scandalized upon observing our parish priest performing the ceremony, and horrified when I realized she was going into labor. Then there was a blackout, and I had to grab Eve's hand and lead her quickly to the exit so she could make her last change. There is nothing blacker than a stage when the lights are suddenly turned off. Things are even worse when the exit door has a board nailed across the top so you have to remember to stoop going out. Poor Eve. She was a tall woman and if I didn't hiss, "duck," at her she invariably forgot, and had to nurse a headache for the rest of the show.

Eve had done the part before and knew what she needed in the way of wardrobe. In fact, she already had her "baby," a pillow-like affair that was elastic and fit like a girdle. We christened it "Junior," of course. She had brought the dresses she wanted to wear, too, but they had to be altered to go around junior. We had trouble with one dress. She had to look pregnant, but had the usual actress's dread of looking fat. The dress was made of a knit fabric that would stretch to cover the "baby", but there was a wide belt. Of course, she didn't have a waistline so she insisted on wearing the belt above the baby bulge. It looked a little strange when, as the scene progressed, the tightness of the belt caused Junior to slip gradually downwards.

In her last scene, Eve has supposedly had her baby and makes her final entrance in a slim white woolen suit. On opening night we were both nervous because of the fast change, (and also, because of my sensational walk on, I had allowed poor Eve to crack her head smartly on the board over the exit door.)

We forgot to remove Junior.

Thank goodness the suit was too tight to go over him. Choking to keep from laughing out loud, we managed to get him off barely in time for her entrance. It would have certainly puzzled the audience to see her still pregnant after suffering with her through her labor pains.

During rehearsal week, Eve and I went shopping for some shoes for her. I hadn't yet discovered how easy she was to get along with, and wasn't looking forward to the trip. Stage shoes must fit well and be easy to move in. I'd shopped with actresses who'd spent hours trying on shoes, sometimes embarrassing me by being rude to the salespeople. Not so, Eve. She tried on one pair of shoes, liked them, and brought four more pairs just like them in different colors. The whole transaction took about fifteen minutes, and the sales ladies were under her spell when we left.

Brooks, to make a terrible pun, I remember barely. He was a lovely man, friendly and easy to get along with. Because the downstairs were so stuffy, the doors were usually left open. By now, I was so used to seeing actors in their undies, I no longer noticed. One night, however I walked into Brooks' dressing room to ask him a question, and there he was, in the buff—completely. He wasn't in the least embarrassed and was gracious enough to ignore my confusion. At some time I'd heard that in such a situation you should look into the person's eyes as you talked. I tried, but oh, it was difficult. I got out of there quickly, my face burning.

Under Papa's Picture was one of the happiest shows I ever worked on. The actors seemed to sincerely like one another, and instead of jealousy and back-biting, there was helpfulness and fun. Eve and Brooks were both so willing to share their years of experience and know-how with the younger actors, and it was so calm that no matter what happened there was no tension backstage —and that's unusual. Even our language improved. Somehow, we just didn't need to swear.

I am afraid we reverted to our bad habits once Eve and Brooks were gone. The following show was such a stinker that even the nice wardrobe mistress went around muttering nasty things, but *Papa Picture* was great while it lasted. We hated to say goodbye to it.

On closing night, Eve gave me a beautiful book, kissed me, and promised to send me a postcard from Mallorca, which she did. Brooks gave me an autographed picture, kissed me, and winked.

Oh dear, I was hoping he'd forgotten.

A Guy and a Doll

Jim Burrows, who directed many of our shows, was determined to do *Guys and Dolls* despite the fact that it's a big musical, and we had a small theater. Also, a "period" musical show needs a costume designer, and we didn't have one.

"You can do it, Trina," said Jim confidently. "It's not a difficult show to costume."

He then proceeded to give me a "little list."

There would be twenty-four people in the cast, and at least half of them would play more than one role. Joe might be a policeman in the prologue, a gangster in scene three, and turn up as a Calypso dancer in the second act. Ginger would spend a lot of time in her dressing room (or the wings) changing her costume, and her personality—from Salvation Army lass, to sloppy waitress, a hooker, and back again. This doubling up of roles is prevalent in small theaters. It costs management less and doesn't require as much dressing room space. It means headaches and lots of lists for the costumer, though.

Thank God for thrift shops. The only nice thing about the location of our theater was the abundance of Goodwill, Salvation Army, and Volunteers of America thrift stores in the vicinity. I was able to find double-breasted suits with wide lapels, terrible ties, and even some wide-band hats for my gangster types. By adding colored shirts, bright hat bands, and pocket handkerchiefs that were color-coordinated with the sets, I was able to make *Guys and Dolls* like a musical instead of a collection of "poor souls.'

I shopped every day and sewed every night—sometimes all night. The dancers' costumes had to be designed and built—four blue and white checked "farmerette" costumes, complete with blue hats and shoes with daisies. I even had to make the daisies, since none of the commercial ones would work.

Another dance number, *Take Back Your Mink*, called for form-fitting black satin gowns that had to be built so they could be removed quickly and easily on stage, revealing black and pink corselets underneath. My ingenuity was also tasked with producing four mink stoles!

"But, remember the budget," Jim reminded me.

How could I ever forget it? It was so small!

Luck was on my side this time. I found some rich-looking fake fur that looked like mink, lined it with satin, and made all four stoles for less than forty dollars.

Another "little" item on my list was six uniforms like those the Salvation Army workers wore in the 1940s.

I'd have to call the Salvation Army. I approached the telephone in my usual cowardly way, convinced that whoever answered would be mean, growl, and reduce me to a nervous wreck. I'd been warned that they wouldn't lend me anything, that other theaters had tried to borrow things and failed, and that the Salvation Army didn't approve of show business or "show people."

The voice on the phone couldn't have been nicer. "Come and talk to me, and we'll see what we can do."

Her name was Lucy, a sweet-faced young woman who listened with interest as I explained what I needed. She was delighted to meet and talk with someone connected with show business and assured me she'd help all she could.

"You'll have to talk to our commander," she said, "but I'm sure he'll do all he can."

Well, after all my worrying, it was so easy. The

commander was a handsome, white-haired man who listened to my story and then arranged for me to borrow, not rent, all the old uniforms I needed.

"They're not in the best of shape," he said, "but I think they'll be all right on stage."

I asked him if he minded them being used in a musical comedy. He assured me that he approved of *Guys and Dolls*, had seen it before, and did I think maybe I could get him a couple of tickets? Not only that, but he said if it was all right with us that each Sunday evening, when their band marched through town, they'd stop in front of the theater and play for the people waiting in line for tickets. Of course, we agreed. It was good publicity and the patrons loved it. You can be sure the kindly man got his tickets—and some for Lucy as well.

Help for *Guys and Dolls* also came from the wonderful Johnson family. Bob and Frances Johnson had owned the theater for years when it was a burlesque house. I've known them for a long time since my father had worked as a drummer for their shows. Their daughter, Dee Ann, was a dancer and actress and was in all of our musicals. Her husband, Tony, was the assistant stage manager for a number of shows and also did small parts. We teased Tony a lot about how often he played a policeman, fireman, or drunk. Playwrights are always sticking in a policeman, a fireman, and drunks, and Tony grew adept at wearing a uniform, or burnt cork and baggy pants.

I sincerely liked the whole Johnson family, not only because of their friendliness, but also because they had all the costumes from the burlesque stored in a small room next door to the theater, and I was always welcome to borrow anything I needed. Every time we did a musical I could usually find something useable in the Johnsons' cubbyhole.

Maureen Reagan, the daughter of Ronald Reagan, then governor of California, and actress Jane Wyman, is a real "doll" to work with. She was a friendly, outgoing girl, and the only actress who spent the time she wasn't on stage down on her knees, cutting out her own costumes.

Maureen Reagan

Maureen played the role of Adelaide, the soft-hearted nightclub dancer, and needed four outfits, one of them a wedding gown, in addition to her dance costumes. Instead of complaining about having to wear the ugly 40's length, the "new" look, Maureen shopped the thrift stores with me whenever she had time and helped me build the things we couldn't find.

About noon the day before dress rehearsal, I realized we weren't going to be able to find a dress suitable for the wedding scene. It would have to be built. I got the fabric, cut out the dress, and had it basted so I could fit it on Maureen after rehearsal. Bless her. She offered to stay and help even though she was so tired she looked gray. The last couple of rehearsals of a show, especially musicals, are ghastly things. The tension and pressure is almost unbearable for everyone, tears flow and tempers fly.

"Go home and get some rest, Luv," I told her. "It'll get done—trust me." I wasn't sure I could really do it, but she had to perform the next day, I didn't.

I finished the dress at 5:00 A.M. it shouldn't have

taken that long, but I was so tired I had to keep doing things over again. I flopped down on the cot Fred, our beloved janitor, doorman, and handyman, had put up in dressing room number two. He knew I wouldn't have time to drive home. My head ached; my back felt like it was broken in three places; and my brain kept buzzing with things still to be done. I felt terribly sorry for myself, alone in the dark, empty theater. I was tired, achy, unloved, and unappreciated. I slept restlessly for a couple of hours, then got up, washed my face, dragged a comb through my awful hair and started to go again— daisies—damned horrid, white and yellow daisies for the "bushel and a peck" dance number.

When Maureen arrived for the morning rehearsal, she found me sitting in dressing room number one (I was using it for a sewing room) laughing like an idiot, with two large daisies fastened to my ample bosom and one in my hair. She looked as if she thought I'd lost my reason, then began to laugh, too. Suddenly everything was all right again. She tried on the dress. It fit beautifully and she loved it, and me. The day before opening was typically dress rehearsal day, frantic, but somehow, early that morning, I had managed to dress myself in a mental suit of armor and was able to help solve all the last minute problems that nervous actors always fall prey to.

Art Metrano played the role of Nathan Detroit in *Guys and Dolls*. He was a good actor, but he and I disliked each other on sight. Maybe he'd had problems with other wardrobe people, I don't know, but he met me with a chip-on-the-shoulder attitude that was demoralizing.

Up to the point of my introduction to Art, I'd always been treated with liking and respect by the actors I'd worked with. I couldn't understand his attitude. He "dared" me to costume him. As I stood with my hand out and a friendly "Hi" ready, he ignored both and snarled.

"I gotta have two good suits, kid—ones that really fit nice. I gotta have stuff that fits good. I can't work in stuff that don't fit. Ya better rent the ones I wore for *The Chicago Teddy Bears* (an ill-fated television show that didn't last long). They fit me right. I ain't got the time to stand around being fit."

What a heartwarming introduction. We were off to a beautiful start. I immediately got the shakes. I wrote all his orders down in my notebook, the hats that "gotta fit good – I got a big head," (did he ever!); the shirts had to be yellow, "long sleeves, two just alike, I sweat a lot," (me too); a blue bow tie, a red turtleneck sweater (that was fun to find—he was built like a blimp), a formal tailcoat and top hat, etc.

Timidly I asked him if he had any suitable shoes. I always asked that. We were primarily of stock theater which meant that actors were required to furnish any clothes they had that might be right for the show.

"Hell, no, I won't wear my own shoes. It'd wreck 'em. You'll just have to buy me some. This is a period show, ain't it? You gotta furnish my stuff. It's union rules."

Of course I knew we had to furnish the clothes if they were forties style. But the two-toned shoes he needed were back in style and I had hoped—ah, well, forget it, Trina. I could see three-quarters of my infinitesimal budget being spent on this one rude man.

It got worse. He seemed to think I was doing my best to destroy him, costume-wise.

"I wear size 17 shirts."

I got size 17 shirts—too tight in the collar.

"These ain't 17's. They must've marked 'em wrong."

I ventured to tell him that 17 ½ might be more comfortable.

"I always wear a seventeen," he bellowed. "These damn things are marked wrong. I wear size 17." He was adamant.

Well, I'd already had a few lessons in diplomacy. When you work with actors, it's necessary to "keep one's cool," so I exchanged the shirts for size 17 ½ and, with a Q-tip, bleached out the one-half mark on the collars.

"See," he said triumphantly, "I toldja I was right. Ya can't trust them fuckin' stores."

I didn't argue. I didn't have time, and it wouldn't have done any good.

He was happy. He'd been right.

I managed to rent the clothes he had worn in the television show. The costume company charged us $50.00 rental fee, but it was a relief to me if something would satisfy Mr. Metrano.

They were too tight.

"Ya sure these are the same ones—they're kinda tight."

I didn't tell him he'd probably put on some weight. Oh no, not me.

"Well, maybe I put on a little around the gut."

Had I heard right? Was he actually admitting it? Was he, maybe, human after all?

"Let the seams out. They feel like hell."

Hateful man. I let the seams out.

Being a coward and hating ugly scenes and rough language, I avoided Art whenever possible. It was easy. During two weeks of rehearsals, he never set foot downstairs.

By the time the show went on, Art had managed to upset everybody. His leading lady was in tears at least once every rehearsal. The crew avoided him whenever possible, and I was ready to give up "show biz." Our little flower from The Bronx was a good actor, but miserably incapable of getting along with people.

Then came opening night.

I had my small workspace downstairs, where most of the dressing rooms were. Art dressed in the "star" dressing room upstairs. There'd been a dust-up over that too, Art insisting on having one of the two large rooms to himself, which meant that John Saxon, actually the male lead in the show, had to dress in the other. This meant the leading ladies, also two, had to dress downstairs—and don't think there isn't a caste system in the theater. The ladies were very sweet about it, but hard feelings were rampant, and Art never set foot downstairs.

Anyway, on opening night I was doing some mending. As the applause died after the first act I heard a small voice say,

"Trina, can you fix this?"

There was Art, a quiet, scared-looking Art, standing there looking white and embarrassed. He turned around and I saw what the problem was. There was a jagged rip in the seat of his pants. In fact the pocket had been completely torn out and his red plaid jockey shorts were exposed to the world.

"Where's the rest of it?" I asked. I felt like a mother interrogating a small naughty boy as he stood there, his giant ego deflated, asking for my help.

"Jesus, I don't know – maybe it's still on the doorjamb on the set. It got caught on the God damn door—uh, sorry."

Was he really apologizing for his language? I suddenly felt sorry for him. Maybe under all that bluster was a nice man.

I had to do something. He had decided to wear only one suit and sent the other one back. I ran upstairs and found the missing piece of fabric. When I got back down, I realized he was near panic.

"Well, give me those pants, and I'll see what I can do. Thank goodness, it's intermission."

"But it's only fifteen minutes, and I'm on right at the beginning of the next act." The poor thing was really scared. "Can you fix it?"

"Sure, I'll send 'em up to you in time." I must've sounded a lot more confident than I felt, because he trotted upstairs looking a lot more cheerful.

I got busy on the patch job and, thanks to the invention of iron-on mending tape, was nearly through when Art came quietly down the stairs.

"Can I help at all?" he asked. He'd wrapped a towel around his waist, although I could have told him the sight of red plaid jockey shorts no longer embarrassed me.

"Thanks—but I'm nearly done."

He sat down on the stairs and watched me work. He also asked questions about me, about my work, my husband, and my children. And he seemed truly interested.

The music was beginning for the second act as I snipped the last thread and handed him his trousers.

"You're a doll," he said as he put them on. "I can't even tell they were torn." Not only was his voice quiet but, strangely, his English had improved a hundred percent. "Thanks." He kissed me and took off down the hall.

Well, I'd like to say that everything changed after that, but it didn't. Art continued to insult people, tell loud, dirty stories, and act like a spoiled child.

But not to me. Somehow I'd gotten under that blustery skin and every single night for the rest of the run Art Metrano came downstairs to pat my shoulder and say "hello" before the show started. And there was never another complaint about his costumes. He never even asked me to replace that suit, but wore it patched for the rest of the run.

Only once, upon seeing a notice on the bulletin

board, a note asking for blood donors for a crew member's sick nephew, did Art let us get a glimpse of the real man. He insisted that we do something about it, and give blood, for the "poor little guy."

Costuming

I'll never know if I was destined to become a costumer or just fell into it because of dance lessons. I always have loved performing and wearing sparkly outfits.

I started to choreograph, or setting dances, when I was about ten and bullied the neighborhood children into "doing a show." Of course we needed costumes, and crêpe paper seemed the easiest to use. That was the beginning for me.

Mother was a talented seamstress, but didn't have the patience to teach me. She did, however, allow me to use her small Singer sewing machine. I taught myself to sew "my" way. I never learned to follow a pattern until many years later when I went to work for a yardage shop and had to make model garments. It was necessary for me to exactly follow Butterick and Vogue patterns. Oh, it was difficult for me, after doing things my own way for years.

Actually, as far as the costuming went, my self-taught method turned out to be just what was needed. Theater work is never slow and methodical. Costume problems happen often instantly, and many times on stage. Actors learn to cover mistakes, whether in their actions or wardrobe dysfunctions, and the costumer backstage must be ready to fix things the minute the actor exits.

Luckily, most problems are discovered during dress rehearsal, the first time the actors perform in costume. Then it's often an all-night session with the sewing machine. At least, though exhausting, it's easier on the nerves than the "instant fixing," I had done for Art Metrano.

I did have twenty-four hours to shorten a dress for the lead dancer in *Paint Your Wagon* being performed by Starlight Opera. I brought this on myself. I was hired to choreograph the show, but the costume they rented for the big can-can number was so awful we all hated it. It was too late to try to find a better one, so I told the producer I'd make the dress if they'd buy the material. I wasn't just being nice. I'd be able to keep the costume when the show was over.

Everybody was happy. I found a beautiful black velvet and red-orange taffeta and sewed all night—then sat and watched the dress rehearsal where my lovely little can-can dancer, in a dress that was too heavy, did a series of spins and twirled herself off the stage and into a surprised drummer's lap. Talk about excitement!

Of course, I had to shorten the skirt before the next night, and believe me, shortening a skirt that was a circle and a half of taffeta-lined velvet with ruffles was no joke. I did get it done, though, and I used the costume for years, then sold it to a costumer in Los Angeles. Luckily I had made it to last.

I think the most fun for me was when the producer complemented me warmly and said, "We didn't know you could sew too."

Charlie Was My Darlin'

Jo Anne Worley

People often ask, "Who is your favorite actor, or actress?" It's impossible for me to pick only one or two favorites. I worked with so many nice, friendly people. It's easier to name the ones I didn't like because there were only a few.

One of my very favorite ladies, however, was Jo Anne Worley. She's a big woman, outspoken, friendly, and fun to be with. She wears fake eyelashes an inch long, fake hair piled high on her head, and incredible clothes. One of my favorite dresses was a long, form-fitting sheath—with horizontal stripes and wild colors. No one could've gotten away with it but Jo Anne. Her personality is so vivid that you expect her clothes to match.

Jo Anne was to do the lead in *Goodbye Charlie*, a play about a man who dies and comes back as a woman, though still thinking and feeling like a man. It's a funny play, but *Charlie* has to make you believe she's a "he" and still look feminine. Jo Anne proved that she is not just a good comedienne, but also an excellent actress. She dropped all the mannerisms she used on television and became *Charlie*.

Jo Anne's costumes had to be feminine, but not too much. She needed a long nightgown and a negligee that was frilly and fuzzy, but not transparent. Instead of sending me out to look for it, she offered to go shopping with me so she could try things on.

Beverly Sanders, the other woman in the play, also needed some things, so the three of us went to our biggest shopping center. What fun trip that was! Jo Anne and Beverly swept through the stores, charming the salespeople, buying armloads of clothes and cosmetics, and making everyone laugh. Jo Anne was recognized, of course, and people followed us about to watch her. She signed autographs graciously. Beverly, instead of being jealous, teased Jo Anne unmercifully.

"It's the eyelashes, honey," she teased. "They just sweep people up like flies."

Both ladies got so carried away with their shopping that I had to remind them that we were looking primarily for a wardrobe for the show.

"You're right," said Jo Anne. "I have to find that silly negligee, don't I?" Then, spotting an unbelievable dress, she grabbed it and headed for the dressing room. "Be right back," she called over her shoulder.

In the meantime, Beverly had disappeared in the opposite direction to look at shoes. When I finally got them rounded up —Jo Anne lugging another box—I tried to be very severe. We had to find a negligee, I told them.

"You're right," said Jo Anne, as she took off like a rocket toward the lingerie department with Beverly and I trailing breathlessly behind. She stopped at a rack of negligees, reached for a blue one, and said, "How about this? It's great. I love it. It's so tacky. Let's buy it, okay?"

We bought it. I wish my shopping was always so easy.

I had been worrying about a "feather dress" described

in the script. Where in the world was I going to find a dress made of feathers? I remembered one of the colleges had produced *Goodbye Charlie*, so I arranged to borrow a dress they had made. Then I met Jo Anne and realized it would be much too small – and how do you alter a dress made of feathers?

Again, I worried too much ahead of time but when I mentioned the feather dress to Jo Anne, she said, "I hope you haven't been worrying about the feather dress. I got something we can use."

She had brought a red dress and a large feather boa to trim it with. It took a while to sew the feathers on, but it looked great when finished. The audience loved it when *Charlie* returned after his first shopping trip as a woman dressed in an improbable creation of red jersey and feathers and a large matching feather hat.

One of Jo Anne's changes was so fast we had to do it right offstage, and during a blackout. I had a flashlight that I had "borrowed" from the stagehands so we could see what we were doing. She not only had to change into the nightgown and negligee, but put on make-up before her entrance. We choreographed the change and it went beautifully until one night I picked up the flashlight and all the insides fell out, making a terrible racket leaving us in the black, black dark. There was nothing to do but make the change by "feel." We did it, but Jo Anne made a comment afterward that it was a strange feeling to make an entrance with no idea if the lipstick was on her mouth, nose, or chin, hoping her eyes didn't look crossed, and wondering if the negligee was on backwards.

Another night during the change, she whispered urgently, "Where's my slippers?"

In her dressing room, that's where. Right where her careless dresser had left them. Pre-setting clothes for the actors' quick changes demands an alert brain. That night mine was fuzzy.

There was no time for me to get them. She did make the entrance barefooted but needed the slippers later in the scene.

"I'll stick 'em in behind the bed," I hissed at her, and ran for the dressing room. I knew she'd have to do some fancy improvising to get the slippers, but that was the only place I could put them where I wouldn't be seen by the audience.

Not to worry. She stuck the ad-lib in snugly between her lines. "I can't find my damn slippers. What have you done with them?" Meanwhile, she was looking behind all the furniture.

"Ah, I knew it." She found them behind the bed where I pushed them under the curtain, sat down, and put them on while returning smoothly to the lines that belonged in the play. Of course, the leading man, Roger Perry, didn't know what was going on, but, dear man, he played right along and the audience thought it was all part of the show.

Roger is the kind of actor people recognize by face instead of by name. A fine performer, capable of playing leading men, heavies, or character roles, he is much in demand and is often seen on television. Actors like Roger are seldom known by name because they have the ability to "become" the person they're portraying. Many stars are good actors, but you're always conscious of who you're watching. Roger Perry is never Roger Perry. He's a family friend, a crooked lawyer, a crooked politician, and equally believable in each part. He's a multi-talented man—actor, musician, composer, writer, and does it all well. He's also delightful to work with, quiet and gentle, but with a wonderful sense of fun. And intelligent? Well, he's the only actor I've ever worked with who had ad-libbed the word "ramifications" in place of a small word he'd forgotten.

Closing night of *Goodbye Charlie*, Jo Anne and Roger had dinner in her dressing room between the matinee and evening performances. Some sliced tomatoes and a mound of potato salad were left over, so she wrapped them in plastic and placed the package in the suitcase Roger was supposed to unpack on stage.

We watched his reaction from the wings. He didn't crack a smile, but lifted the mess out of the suitcase and said, "I see my salad's still okay." Then he continued to unpack. We awarded him a gold star for "uncrackability."

The cast of Goodbye Charlie

Another Charlie and His Aunt

The show that most taxed my patience, ingenuity, temper, and mental health was *Charlie's Aunt*. The story takes place about 1900, the turn-of-the-century. It was a period of elegance with satins, laces, flounces, and ruffled parasols for the ladies and frock coats, striped trousers and high silk hats for the men.

One of our local theaters had produced the play three years before, so I was able to rent many things I needed. Not enough, though. Again, I had to sew into the early morning hours to get the show ready.

To begin with, the first week of rehearsal took place in Los Angeles. That meant I had to produce costumes that would fit reasonably well and all I had to go by was a list of measurements. Measurements can be tricky, especially when the actors are allowed to write their own lists. I learned the hard way to always add an inch to every lady's bust and waist measurements, and to subtract the same amount from the men's chest expansion claims. Even that wasn't enough for one of the actresses. Talk about fibs! She sent me her vital statistics—36-26-37. I found two satisfactory dresses. Then I met her. I tried to squeeze her into them but she was on the plus side of 39-28-37— too large by far for the costumes. I let out seams as far as I could go. No go. I borrowed more dresses. She didn't like them. I spent hours building her a new costume. When it was half-done, she tearfully informed me without even seeing it that she wanted a "professional" dress. It was a good thing I was too tired to say what I really thought. I just sat and looked at her thinking how hard to please and bulgy she was. After costuming dozens of actors and actresses and making clothes for people like Dorothy Lamour and Kaye Ballard, I consider myself professional.

Oh well it was 2:00 a.m. and dress rehearsal would start at 10:00 a.m. I would have loved to see her have to perform start-naked, but it was my job to furnish her with a costume.

In desperation I grabbed one of the borrowed dresses she didn't like, let out seams, added ruffles, flowers, lace, everything I could find. She was happy, but I'm ashamed to admit she did a whole act every night in a ball dress when she should have been wearing a daytime outfit. She did not know the difference and by then I didn't care.

The most important costume in the play is a long black dress the male star wears when impersonating *Charlie's Aunt*. It has to be specially made, not only because it must fit a man, but also because there is so much stage "business" connected with it. He/she slides across tables, dances, and, at one point, does a running swan dive into the dress while it's being held by Charlie and his friend, Jack. It has to be made to "breakaway" so he can get in and out of it quickly. The skirt must be very full and weighted at the bottom so it will move well.

Louis Nye

In one scene, "Auntie," is handed a bunch of flowers.

"What'll I do with them?" he/she asks.

"Stick 'em down your dress," is the answer, so there has to be a long, narrow pocket sewn to the outside of the bodice for that purpose. Also required is a full-length ruffled petticoat with elastic suspenders.

Louis Nye was to be our star. He had done the show many times before, and the rental agency in New York had the costume he had worn. Hurray! I wouldn't have to worry about it. I felt so relieved that I got brave and called the rental place all by myself. Clear to New York! Me! I arranged to rent the dress, and they promised to send it right away so we'd have it for publicity pictures.

I believed them. I trusted them. I waited patiently, then nervously. I called New York again.

It's on its way," a syrupy voice assured me. "Should be there by tomorrow."

I waited two more days. I began to feel panicky. I called again.

"I don't understand." It was the same voice. "It should be there by now." I hated that calm, blah person, whoever she was. She continued, "I took it to the air freight office myself."

I called our freight office. "Sorry, it's not here."

Louis was expected in Los Angeles the next day, and the newspaper photographers would be there in the afternoon. I was supposed to drive up early in the morning with the dress.

What could I do? I told Jim Burrows, the director, if the pictures could be taken from the waist up I'd try to come up with a suitable bodice. He gave me a picture of Louis that had been taken during another production.

I improvised. It was too late to buy anything so I had to make do with what I had on hand. I took a black shirt that John Saxon had worn in *Guys and Dolls*, turned the collar in, and sewed white lace to the neck and cuffs. In the picture Louis was wearing a white lace shawl. Our prop department lost a lace curtain.

Thank heavens Louis had promised to bring his own

wig, so I didn't have to worry about that. I finished my makeshift outfit about 1:00 a.m. and went home to dream about Mr. Nye's reaction when I told him his dress hadn't come. I always worry about terrible things that never happen. When I was introduced to the talented man whose face and marvelous characterizations have been a by-word since the early *Steve Allen Show*, I told him about what had happened.

"Don't worry," he smiled as he shook my hand. "I'm sure it'll work fine."

I was his willing slave from then on.

After the pictures were taken, Jim and Louis asked me if I could build a special dress. The first performance was only three days away and obviously we couldn't wait for the lost costume to "maybe" be found.

"I'll do it," I said, "if someone else will call the rental company and cancel the order. I won't call them again."

Can you imagine? I've never before been able to say "won't."

Jim agreed to do the phoning and I felt liberated. He told me later that when he called they were still looking for the dress.

Louis had pictures of the costume and knew all the tricky things it needed. He was very patient during fittings and, even though he remembered things he needed after the dress was already sewn up, he was so diplomatic about it that I cheerfully did things over, and cheerfully doing things over is not one of my virtues. Louis had a way of complementing me and asking me to change something at the same time.

"That's no problem, Louis," I assured him. "I'll just add some more skirt."

No problem? What was the matter with me? Of course it was a problem. It necessitated taking the whole thing apart and adding pieces of fabric to the skirt. See what I mean? I did it graciously, no grumbling, no tears.

It was the middle of night before the final rehearsal when I finished the dress and started on the petticoat. At least I intended to start on the petticoat. Guess who had been so busy she had forgotten to buy the fabric? I don't think Louis ever knew the long ruffled petticoat was made out of two white sheets – as far as I know, the prop department never missed them. Louis tried on the petticoat the next morning. "It's just fine." He twirled around in it. "It really feels right." I felt warm with pride, then... "Would it be too much trouble to dye it gray? My other ones have always been gray. It looks better on stage." He looked worried.

"Of course not. I'll just throw it into my washer." Sure I would. When? In my spare time, between three and five in the morning, that's when. But I didn't say it.

Actors, take note. It's amazing what a little sugar will do when dealing with a wardrobe mistress.

Sometimes it's debatable whether an article of clothing is a costume or prop. Usually it depends on whether it is worn or just used. In *Charlie's Aunt* we needed a top hat that was both. One of the actors had to wear it, but it also had to have tea and cream and sugar poured into it every night. Obviously, an ordinary hat wouldn't do. We couldn't use an old hat, either, because it had to look expensive when worn.

I found an almost-new top hat that was the right size, then turned it over to the prop department to experiment on, along with my promise of instant death to all if they ruined it. It had cost me $25, and, top hats being hard-to-find, not too easy to replace in a hurry. They worked on it for days, trying every way they could think of to make it waterproof without spoiling the outside. It also had to be fixed so it would pour a certain way—a small, steady stream instead of a splashy waterfall. It finally worked, although never to Louis' complete satisfaction.

Edgar Daniels, the actor who needed the special hat, was a giant of a man. He was six foot, three inches tall, almost as wide, and had a voice to match. Intelligent and outspoken, he did beautiful needlepoint in his dressing room between scenes.

Because of Edgar's size, I was allowed to rent his costumes from Los Angeles, except, of course, for the top hat. Rental companies don't take kindly to their top hats being returned with the inside coated with layers of resin and a home-made pouring spout. He told me everything had been already altered to fit, so I didn't worry about his wardrobe. I should have. When he put on his first outfit for dress rehearsal, we discovered the vest was so short his ample stomach stuck out between vest and trousers. Ditto for both of his other vests.

Damn!

Well, there was nothing to do but invent something quickly. I made "cheat" vests which were just fronts. They worked fine. Luckily, he wasn't required to remove his coats on stage so the audiences were never subjected to my Rube Goldberg mess of tapes and elastic.

Thank God for lace. I couldn't have costumed *Charlie's Aunt* without it. I used lace to cover new ugly parasols, old torn flounces, and flat bosoms, ancient coffee stains, and ring-around-the-collar. The only problem with Louis's black dress that I never really solved was the collar. Louis wanted a high stiff collar trimmed with white lace. I made the collar all right, but if I used stiff lace it scratched him, and any other kind got limp—and Louis did not like limp lace. He was always so kind about asking me to fix it.

"Just put another ruffle on it," he'd say each night.

There were finally six layers of lace ruffles on the collar, and because it always got makeup on it I had to take the lace off, wash it, and put it back on about every other night.

I used so much lace in *Charlie's Aunt* that it became a theater joke. The prop people finally got the "tea" hat working right, I heard one of them say, "Don't let Trina get hold of it. She'll cover the damn thing with lace."

Sic 'em, Charlie Brown

You're a Good Man, Charlie Brown is a charming, small musical and can be effective. There are traps, however. The audience must believe that six full-grown actors and actresses are really five children and a dog. The set consists of what looks like large wooden building blocks constructed in different shapes and painted in bold primary colors. There are 102 different lighting cues. Audience imagination is responsible for everything else. The story is simply a series of events in one day of Charlie Brown's life, with a blackout at the end of each.

People think it's a children's show and kids love it, but the dialogue, the music, lyrics, and the staging are so clever that an adult "understands" the show, while a child simply enjoys it.

Charles Shultz is a master at bridging the gap between adult and child. His whimsical little characters have become very real to thousands of people, not only in America, but all over the world. However, this popularity is exactly why the musical is risky to produce. Will audiences accept the premise of adults acting as children and animals? We found out they would if there are no stars used. If the people in the audience recognize a well-known actor, the illusion is destroyed. Charlie Brown must be Charlie Brown. And Snoopy is a small black and white dog.

Excitement had begun to build in the theater circles of our town when word got around that no "names" would be used. It sounded as if some of our excellent local talent would finally have a chance. Then the bubble burst.

"I will not even listen to anyone who is taller than five-foot-seven." The director was adamant.

How ridiculous. Another small theater (non-professional) had produced the show the year before and had proven beyond doubt that big people, if good enough actors, could beautifully create the illusion of children. I saw the local production, with a Charlie who was five-foot, ten inches tall, a Linus and Shroeder each five-foot eleven, and a six-foot Snoopy. The show was delightful and believable, so it could be done. Not only that, but we had the actors who had played Charlie, Snoopy, and Lucy working right in our own box office. They were professionals now, belonged to the union, and were doing box office work so they could live between shows.

They weren't even allowed to audition. Everyone in the theater, from the producer to the janitor, tried to get the director to change his mind, but no, he was from New York, had done the show there, and was not going to change his mind.

It took weeks to cast the show. They finally had to send to Boston for a boy who had done the part of Charlie before. And guess how tall he was? Five-foot-ten!

Charlie Brown was not a big success. The actors weren't exceptional and the staging was unimaginative. San Diego audiences had learned to expect famous people in our shows, but I sincerely believe local talent would have surprised them.

From start to (early) closing, the morale was low. The actors did their best, but were not particularly friendly with the crew. The director was difficult to work with. He wanted everything exactly as it had been in New York, which, of course, was his prerogative, but he didn't have the facility to explain what he wanted.

As a result, much had to be done twice, or even three

times. Costume-wise, every actor had to have two of each garment, and those should be exact duplicates of the ones worn in the New York production. This is California and one just doesn't run to the nearest store and buy a long-sleeved woolen turtleneck sweater in May, let alone two. It's also hard to find white patent-leather "Mary Jane" shoes for adults. Our two girls were small, true, but had adult-sized feet.

The day I met the director (mutual dislike at first sight) he grunted something I accepted as a greeting of some sort, then handed me two faded, ragged garments and mumbled, "You'll have to make two of each of these dresses, and they'll need matching panties, white tights, and white patent-leather Mary Jane shoes."

"Okay, how long do you want the dresses?"

"Oh, well, to come to about here." He indicated a point about halfway between his waist and knee. He later decided (after the dresses were finished, of course) that he wanted them two inches longer than four inches shorter. I nearly wore out the fabric re-hemming it. It was the same with the panties. First he wanted fitted short ones, then long bloomers, then finally decided on medium, semi-fitted bloomers, which meant building them all over again–all four pair. Luckily for me, both girls were patient and willing to stand quietly while I fit and refit.

At least I didn't have to build the boys' clothes. Here, it was merely a matter of shopping for hours to find shirts, trousers, sweaters, and shoes to fit small grownups, with, of course, duplicates of everything. Bobby Towers, who played Snoopy, needed two pairs of black stretchy trousers with a 27-inch waist and a 27-inch inseam, not an easy size to find. He also had to have a pair of white tennis shoes, which shouldn't have been any problem, but Bobby had broken a bone in his foot and had to wear the shoes over a bulky bandage. This meant buying over-sized shoes and stuffing one to fit. He was the funniest thing you've ever seen, a tiny man portraying a dog with size twelve feet.

Bobby was my favorite of the Charlie Brown cast. He was one of the few small men I've met who never tried to appear bigger, meaner, and stronger than anyone else. He accepted his size and had spent years perfecting his talent. And he is talented.

One afternoon, during the break between the matinee and evening performances, Bobby asked the cast and crew members if we'd act as an audience for a one-man show he was preparing to entertain school children. It was delightful. He sang, danced, recited poetry, and brought some of Dr. Seuss's characters to life for us. We were all enjoying the show so much we missed dinner, but it was worth it.

Oddly enough, for weeks after the show the words "peanut butter" were enough to send any of the crew into hysterics. In one scene, Charlie eats part of a peanut butter sandwich. He usually only took one bite (it's very difficult to say lines with a mouthful of the stuff) and after the scene the crew would draw straws to see who got the rest of the sandwich. Theater crews are always hungry and will eat practically anything. Closing night of the show some practical joker put a piece of paper in the sandwich, right in the center so it wouldn't show. When Charlie took his bite he missed the paper, but the crew member who drew the short straw didn't. Most of us were in on the joke, and when we realized it hadn't worked on stage, we "arranged" for Wimpy, our head carpenter, to get the rest of the sandwich. He accepted it, stood there calmly eating the whole thing, paper and all, with a completely expressionless face. He thanked us and went back to work.

Everybody's Rose Marie

I had five more sailors in *Everybody's Girl*, suggestive title for an innocuous play, successful only because of the personal magnetism of Rose Marie, an outgoing, big-hearted lady. The cast and crew got along well, making it a pleasure to work.

Outfitting sailors was easy for me by then, but I still had to be careful about insignias. There are dozens of different ones, and woe be onto the costume lady who works in a Navy town like San Diego and uses the wrong one, or sews it on the wrong place. She hears about it in a hurry.

Trouble with my sailors in *Everybody's Girl* was that each one was supposed to be from a different ship in training and a different job, necessitating all kinds of colors of insignias. Also, halfway through the show, the boys come home with their uniforms dirty, bloodied, and torn to shreds after a fight, which meant two uniforms with identical insignia for each boy, one of which had to be ripped and dirty. It sounds easy. "Just tear it up and stuff it into the dirt." In reality, it's difficult to make a garment look realistically old, dirty, and torn. It took a lot of experimenting to come up with something that really looked like dried blood.

Dress rehearsal went well, for a dress rehearsal, and it wasn't until after the opening night performance that I got the message—actually five messages. All the stripes on the uniform sleeves were upside down. So, after the opening night party, I had to go back to the theater, painstakingly remove all the stripes, and sew them back on right.

I hate uniforms.

Rose Marie had her own dresser, a small, energetic English woman named Joy, who, because she was working on a television show, commuted between Hollywood and San Diego every day.

Honestly!

She'd drive to the airport after a day's work at the TV studio and fly to San Diego where she was picked up and brought to the theater just in time for Rose Marie's first change. She'd zip four zippers and fasten a string of pearls, and then make the whole trip in reverse after the show. Of course, I could have helped Rosie with her changes, but she insisted that Joy be included in her contract. The whole thing seemed to me pretty silly, but we liked Rosie and Joy and there were no problems. Well, only one. One night Joy missed her plane and I was suddenly needed.

I had no idea what Rosie's changes were because Joy had been doing them and I had busied myself with the other actors. With Rosie's help, I pre-set her clothes in the wings and got ready for her final change. It went smoothly.

Then, just as she was ready to make her entrance she said, "Ah, my God, I forgot to tell you about the black dress. It's still in the dressing room and I'll need it next."

I took off for the dressing room, nearly breaking a toe on a protruding flat, only to discover she locked the room – and Joy had the key! Good Lord, everything she needed for the rest of the show was in there. I ran looking for Fred, who had the only extra key. No Fred. It was almost time for the next change. In desperation, I grabbed a hammer from the carpenters box was just about to jeopardize my job by breaking an expensive dressing room door when the stage door burst open and Joy came charging through.

She got the dressing room unlocked just in time for Rose's next change and I went and hid behind my water heater to get my breath back, resolving to always know everyone's changes from then on.

Actors are trained to think and act quickly when unforeseen things happen on stage. A play can be spoiled because someone forgets lines or breaks character, and many times an actor is saved by someone else's quick thinking.

One night during the run of *Everybody's Girl*, Rose Marie's zipper came apart when she was on stage. She was unaware of it, but one of the boys standing behind her saw what had happened. He quickly moved to her, put his hand against her bare back so she'd know the zipper was broken and then ad-libbed,

"Gee, Mom, it's getting chilly. I'll get you a sweater." He came offstage, Joy ran for a sweater, and the whole thing was handled so smoothly the audience never knew anything had gone wrong.

Another night the stage manager was careless and the prop phone didn't ring when it was supposed to. Rose Marie ad-libbed a couple of lines and then said, "There must be something wrong with the damn phone again. I've been expecting a really important call."

By that time the stage manager was back on the beam and, although the audience had caught on, they good-naturedly applauded when the phone finally rang.

Red Hot Don Knotts

The minute word got out that Don Knotts was coming to the off-Broadway theater to star in *The Last of the Red Hot Lovers*, the box office phone began to ring, and ring, and ring. The show was completely sold out in a short time and was extended for two weeks because of the heavy demand for tickets. Somehow, the combination of a play written by Neil Simon and performed by Don Knotts, that funny, nervous little man, appealed to the people who usually sat at home, watching TV and eating popcorn.

It was a good play. Don is a fine actor with superb timing and he can make you believe in his character. In *Red Hot Lovers*, one man tries to have an affair with three different women, one in each act, which meant that Don was on stage constantly. It was an exhausting role and he

Don Knotts

was nervous about appearing before a live audience after years of television work. In TV, the scenes are shot one at a time, quite different from a play where the actor must know the whole script and can only relax between acts.

Don wore his own clothes for *Red Hot Lovers* so all I had to do was see that they were kept clean and pressed. Luckily, I liked him because the cleaning and pressing became a chore. He changed clothes during each intermission and dropped everything in a heap. He perspired heavily and always dumped his soaking wet shirt and under shirt right on top of his beautiful custom-made suits. If I wasn't right there to grab them and hang them up, they'd have to be pressed again. I hadn't yet discovered a laundry that would do shirts overnight, so I had to iron three dress shirts and three undershirts every day. Thank goodness we weren't having matinees. I would have had a problem getting things dried between shows.

There was a bit of business in the first act as Don was supposed to take his handkerchief out of his pocket and wipe the actress's face. He was very good about always checking to see if the hanky was there, so after the first couple of performances I stopped worrying about it.

Well, someday I'll learn. One night he didn't check, I didn't check, and when the time came he reached in his pocket and—no handkerchief!

What a quick-thinking man he is. He made a big thing out of looking for the handkerchief, then pulled out his shirttail, ripped a piece off (with difficulty) and handed it to the actress, who was in hysterics by then. The audience loved it. I had to mend the shirt but it served me right. From then on we both checked for the hanky.

Pam Britton was back for *Red Hot Lovers*. She is a favorite with all of us and so easy to work with. It was fascinating to watch her get her way with sweet and quiet diplomacy, quite unlike one of the other actresses who stamped, ranted, and screeched every time something didn't suit her.

"Do you think maybe I would look better standing at this angle?" Pam would ask. With actress number two it came out more like this, "I will not stand like that, dammit, my profile is better on the other side."

Or, Pam would say to me, "You work so hard I hate to ask you for anything more, but do you think I could have a purse that's easier to open?"

Of course she could—I loved the lady.

Number two purred like a kitten and scattered "dahlings" around indiscriminately when she was having her way, but, oh boy, if she was unhappy about something, the nasty four letter words came out in staccato shrieks.

I'm not going to name number two because I'd hate to be the cause of her future unemployment. Poor thing. She's going to have a hard enough time. Nobody who's worked with her will ever want to again. A tall, blonde woman approaching middle-age with great reluctance, she was a pain from the first rehearsal. She believed she was a great actress, and couldn't understand why we never heard of her (I've never heard of her since, either). She was "on" all the time, talking loudly and with an accent we were never able to place. Evidently, she'd invented it herself. Her disposition was a pendulum swinging from sweetie-pie to bitch, and I tried to keep out of her way as much as possible.

We had a running feud over a beautiful, expensive fur coat I had borrowed for her to wear in the show. The coat was worth $2,500 and I was very careful to lock it up each night. She loved that coat. She wasn't in the second or third acts and it disturbed me when I noticed she was wearing the coat in her dressing room while she waited for the curtain call. She chained-smoked and, picturing the beautiful coat with holes burned in it, I spoke to her about it.

"But, dahling, I don't have a robe, and this is so lovely and warm," she purred at me, stroking the fur.

I got a robe out of wardrobe. Oh, the poisonous look I got in return.

I was busy the next few nights and didn't notice she wasn't in her room during the second and third acts.

Then Wednesday one of the crewmembers called me aside. "Hey, you know what the blonde bitch is doin' between acts? She's three-sheetin'. I saw her last night out front."

"Three sheeting" is the term used for the old practice where an actor stood under his picture in the theater lobby during intermissions and waited to be recognized. Today it's considered blatant and unprofessional. Well, that's what she was doing all right. She'd wander around the lobby in stage makeup and my fur coat, graciously accepting compliments from the theater-goers. I couldn't believe it. Not only that, but I discovered she also went next door to the Palace Bar between intermissions and entertained the drinkers by singing blues songs.

When I heard about that I was spitting mad. I went straight to Jim Burrows pointed out what a bind he'd be in, if something happened to the coat.

"You know what kind of neighborhood this is?" I asked him. "She can be replaced, but that fur coat cannot, and we're responsible for it."

He promised to talk to her.

She came to me. "Why did you tattle on me?" she complained and I could hear "you bitch" in her thoughts. "I'm not hurting anything."

I pointed out to her that there was a strict rule about wearing any wardrobe item out of the theater, especially an expensive, borrowed fur coat.

This is a rotten part of town," I told her. "It's not safe."

"I can take care of myself," she said. "I'm not afraid."

"It's not you I'm worried about." I realized it didn't sound very nice, but that time I didn't care.

She pouted the rest of the evening, but that woman

had the hide of a rhinoceros. The following night she asked if she could wear the coat to dinner and seemed honestly surprised when I said "no."

Don Knotts felt the extent of her explosive temper on opening night, as did everyone else backstage. Don was understandably nervous. Opening-night audiences are always full of critics, both the professional and the self-made ones. It was important for the show to get good reviews because they wanted to take it to other cities. If all went well, the actors would have work for the entire summer, and the producers would make money, that marvelous, useful stuff.

The first act began well. The nervousness didn't show until Don inadvertently skipped a line. Ordinarily that doesn't matter much, but that night when the actors tried to cover the mistake they jumped ahead four pages of dialogue.

The audience was unaware of the mistake because the jump was made smoothly and it didn't leave out anything particularly important to the story, just dialogue. But, half of that dialogue belonged to our number two actress. Wow! When the act was over, she came roaring offstage screaming, really screaming! Thank God there was music playing or the whole audience would have heard. Her language was, to say the least, colorful. She stamped downstairs and to her dressing room, slammed the door hard enough to shake the whole theater, and locked it. She had confided to me earlier, and probably to everyone else, that her psychoanalyst had told her not to hold anything in, to "let herself go" when she was angry.

Boy! Did she ever. She screamed, threw things, yelled that "he" had ruined her show. Her show, my hat!

When Don came downstairs and tried to apologize, she wouldn't let him in or even listen to him. It was an exciting evening. She stayed in her room, crying childishly through the rest of the show, and then showed up for the curtain calls with the pouty, blotchy face. She apologized later, but the harm had been done. She lost any respect the cast and crew might've had for her, and from then on we treated her with professional politeness, nothing more.

I'll have to admit, however, that even though unpleasant when she wasn't getting her way, our fiery actress was professional on stage.

The first act of the play—her act—was about a woman who smoked constantly. She was visiting Barney (Don), who not only didn't smoke, but he never kept any cigarettes in his apartment. The whole act revolved around her craving a smoke.

One night some smart-aleck in the audience threw a lighted cigarette on the stage at the beginning of the scene. If either of the actors had even looked at it, the whole act would've been ruined. There they were, she, acting angry and noisily ridiculing, he, nervous, and apologetic, all because he didn't have a cigarette to offer her.

And all the time there on the floor, sending curls of smoke up into their eyes, was the disputed object.

The act seemed endless. You could feel the audience literally holding its breath. Crewmembers crossed fingers and worried.

We needn't have. Both actors ignored the cigarette. Not only that, but when Don had to cross downstage, he made an unnoticeable detour and extinguished the thing with his foot.

Audiences can be coldly cruel, warmly receptive, or wriggly and inattentive, but they're not stupid. The applause at the end of Act I that night was warm with adoration for two professional performers.

The Gypsy in My Soul

When *Storm in Summer* closed, so did the theater. There had been financial problems, trouble with the union, and hints of mismanagement. People muttered darkly in corners, and the morale was low. The business manager told me a week before the end of the show, that we were closing, but were expected to re-open shortly under new management.

The theater did reopen six weeks later. I was asked to come to the staff meeting to meet the new owners and find out about the next show, *Gypsy*.

"My God," I thought. "Here we go again." I love the show—I always have—but it's a musical needing a large cast of lavish costumes. We had a small theater, small dressing rooms, and me.

Don Wortman and Tom Hartzog, the new owners, seemed nice enough. We sat in the theater and listened to their enthusiastic plans for the big reopening. The enthusiasm was contagious and I found myself actually believing we could do *Gypsy*. This allusion was rudely shattered when Don turned to me and said,

"Now, *Gypsy* is a costume show. I'll talk with you later, but I'll give you a partial list to start on." I grabbed my notebook and pencil and proceeded to write another "little list," getting colder and colder, then panicked as I wrote.

A white bunny fur coat, hat, and muffler for Baby June.

An "Uncle Sam" costume for Louise.

Identical Statue of Liberty and Uncle Sam costumes for the two girls who would play the grown-up June and

Louise.

Uniforms, (what else?) for four small boys, a soldier, sailor, marine, and member of the Coast Guard, and identical costumes for four big boys.

Four pseudo-Spanish costumes with awful-looking blonde wigs and black lace mantillas.

Six showgirl costumes like they used to wear at Minsky's, with elaborate headdresses.

Two Santa Claus suits.

Costumes for a Dutch girl and boy.

A rhinestone dress for Baby June.

Four farmer outfits, a farmerette dress.

Four "Broadway" suits with Elton jackets, top hats, and canes,

A cow.

By this time I was numb, just writing things down and trying not to think. When Don saw my face he quickly assured me the cow could be rented. Thank goodness I wouldn't have to make that. It was to be the kind of costume that covered two people, one at the head and one at the tail – and they had to dance in it.

And then, the *piece-de-resistance*: Gypsy Rose would need four "strip" costumes. No problem. Then his words began to penetrate.

"She'll have to start the number wearing all four outfits. There's no time to change. Can you work it out?"

My Lord, he thinks I'm superwoman. Not only that, but he thinks I'm a designer.

But I nodded meekly. I'll never admit there's anything I can't do, and that's a dandy way to get impossible jobs thrown at you.

Well, there were dozens of other things for me to put on my list, but by then I was just writing like a robot, with my brain turned off.

I spent the next two days going over the script and the

list, with thoughts of resigning. It was too much for one person. Who did they think I was? How could anyone expect so much?

After three days of desperate figuring and planning, I went to the theater to get started. I felt scared and helpless. Napoleon had his Waterloo. Trina had her *Gypsy*.

Don was in his office.

"Oh, Trina," he said. "The designer is coming in on the three o'clock plane. Will you meet him?"

Designer? What designer? A costume designer, that's what, only no one had thought to tell me. I was furious, not because I wanted to design the show, not me, but because they let me stew and worry for three days. Then I felt the heavy weight roll off my back as I realized it was the designer's job to worry.

I drove to the airport with mixed feelings. I was glad I would have a real designer, but I also knew I'd be spending fourteen days, and probably nights, working with him. Putting on a show means real togetherness for designer and seamstress and I earnestly hoped we would like each other.

I shouldn't have worried. Joe Thompkins was a small man with a big mustache and a huge talent. He had a Texas drawl and a crazy sense of humor that matched mine. It was instant friendship, and we managed to work together seventeen or eighteen hours a day for fourteen days with no friction, a miracle in the world of show business when everyone works under such pressure that flare-ups are common.

Joe knew his business. He made sketches for me, picked up fabrics, and shopped while I sewed, sewed, and sewed.

I don't like to shop, but I do like the challenge of making a costume look like the sketch.

Joe, unlike many theater designers, could sew too, and at night, when the stores were closed, we accomplished amazing things. He also took on the job of making the headdresses for the "Minsky" showgirl scene. Armed with a hot glue gun and a box full of tinsel, sequins, wire, ribbon, and Christmas tree ornaments, he concocted fantastic Ziegfeld-like creations.

Among our challenges was the designing and making of three coats, including one for a small poodle, that had to look like they were made from the hotel blankets used in the previous scene. That meant finding enough suitable fabric to make the blankets and the coats. We were lucky. We found a loud plaid, blanket-like fabric and were able to get a whole bolt. Also, it was on sale because the plaid was printed slightly crooked. It was all the better for us because the coats are supposed to look a little weird anyway. After all, teen-aged "Louise" had made them from pilfered hotel blankets.

It was a show-stopping scene when, one by one, Mama Rose, Louise, and dainty Jane entered in identical coats – with Louise carrying a tiny black poodle, also in a matching coat. The laughter would start because the coats were made in the style of the twenties, short, pleated in back, with wide satin, low slung sashes, and they looked funny. Then suddenly, as the audience realized they were made out of the blankets, the laughter would build and build. It's a good feeling when your costumes get that kind of response.

Joe and I were both nervous about Kaye Ballard's costumes. She was to play the part of Mama Rose and would need five outfits. She was supposed to look pretty tacky in the first part of the show when they're poor, but quite elegant at the end, and, because the show is set in the twenties and thirties, everything would have to be built. We had heard through the grapevine that she was hard to please, and we didn't have much time.

That should've warned us that there'd be problems, but we were so relieved when she approved the sketches, and so mesmerized by her likable personality that we didn't worry.

Kaye Ballard

Joe made sketches for each outfit and had them ready when she came downstairs from the first day of rehearsal. She loved them, and we loved her. Outgoing, loud, and friendly, she made some suggestions for a few changes, but tactfully. She was a heavy set woman, and very conscious of it, so it was our job to build costumes she'd be comfortable in, could sing in, and would feel thinner in. She warned us that she hated to stand for fittings, and asked that we do it all in one day

Two days before the show was to open I had her dresses ready for fitting. It had been hard just working from measurements, and I had my fingers crossed. She tried them all on, liked them, but informed me that she didn't like to wear a slip, and they'd all have to be fully lined – weird!

Goddamn. There's nothing that's more of a nuisance than lining a garment already put together. We knew by this time that her word was law. The star must be pleased, so I spent the night lining her dresses, and using some of my recently acquired "theater language."

Joe, the beast, laughed at me until he was limp, not because of the lining job (he was sympathetic about that) but because of my language.

Linda Kaye Henning

People always laughed when I swore. I guess I just didn't look like anything but a middle-aged, plump grandmother. I tartly pointed out that I'd learned quite a few of my new epitaphs from *him*. They have some dandy words in Texas.

When I first saw Linda Kaye Henning's measurements I thought someone had made a mistake. No one could have a twenty-one inch waist.

Linda did.

She was a tiny quiet, sweet-voiced girl with the patience of a saint. She was to portray Gypsy Rose Lee and would have to wear the four strip costumes. The only way we could make them fit right was to practically build one on top of the other—on Linda. What a love! Anytime she wasn't rehearsing, she was standing patiently in the number two dressing room having pins stuck in her by two tired, fumble-fingered costumers.

It was worth the effort. On opening night, the three of us, Linda, Joe, and I, basked in the warm, loud applause as Gypsy made her entrance in a form-fitting black crêpe gown and a fur stole. She paraded around as she sang, then exited, only to re-enter five seconds later dressed in an orange, sequin-decorated, satin gown, also skintight. She repeated the exit and quick re-entrance, this time wearing a short, red glittering corselet trimmed with fringe and carrying a huge red ostrich-plume hat. Her last outfit consisted of white sequined bikini panties, a white fox fur stole, and an elaborate headdress. We had a little more time for the last change, but it was still fast, fast, fast, and hooray for Velcro. I never saw the number from the front—I was too busy with the changes—but from the audience reactions it was spectacular. Joe and I got a lot of compliments, and questions, about that number.

The show was to open in three days. It was four a.m. when Joe and I admitted to each other that we had to have some help if we expected to get finished in time. We sat in dressing room number two, surrounded by piles of fabric. Many garments were done, but there were still a lot that were only cut out, and some not even started yet. We were in trouble. It's difficult to find people who know how to sew for the stage as it's very different from dressmaking. Everything must look good from the front but has to be made in a hurry. There are a lot of shortcuts, but never enough time to teach them to the helpers. It's also hard to find people who are willing to sew for twelve or thirteen hours at a stretch for a small amount of money. Especially, in our case, if they are claustrophobic. I was able, through friends, to find three dear ladies who not only sewed for days but put up with my tired snappiness and stayed constantly cheerful. They adored Joe, who has the wonderful ability to stay nice under stress, and luckily, they liked me, too, because I get crabby when I go too long without sleep. Kay, Sally, and Anna helped us finish the show. We couldn't have done it without them.

At 6:00 p.m. on the last day, Joe walked into the dressing room where we had three sewing machines, a dozen finished costumes hanging from the ceiling, scraps and pins ankle-deep on the floor, and four tired ladies staring dully at each other. Kay and he and I had spent the day making a new costume for Kaye Ballard because she and Joe had changed their minds about her final outfit. Sally and Anna had spent the whole day doing the tiresome little finishing jobs: hems, hooks, eyes, and snaps.

Joe stood in the doorway. His eyes were red, he hadn't shaved – even his mustache drooped – but he had a bottle of champagne in his hand that Kaye had given us days before that we hadn't had time to drink.

"Hey, my sweet 'lil'ol' sewin' ladies," he said. "We are done. How about that? How about we celebrate? Trina-May, you got any cups?"

We found some paper cups, toasted each other with warm champagne, and then finished the whole bottle. I very seldom drink, not liking the taste of alcohol, but I was tired and the room was hot and stuffy. All I remember about the next two hours was a lovely, floating feeling, being laughed at by everyone, and Joe and Kay trying to sober me up by insisting I eat something.

Luckily, I was all right by the time dress rehearsal started.

Boy, what a night. I knew there would be a lot of quick costume changes' and Kay and another old friend, Maybelle, had promised to help me, but we'd been so busy sewing no one had time to figure out where and when the changes were.

I got the cast together and asked them to help.

"All of you know what's been happening around here," I told them. "You've all got costumes, but we have no idea when you change. Tonight you'll have to help us. If you have a quick change, pre-set your costume, and when it's time, come offstage yelling for help quietly. One of us will be there. By tomorrow we will have them all planned so it's only tonight that there's a problem, okay?"

We survived dress rehearsal. It was pure bedlam backstage. There were fifteen some changes, so there was a lot of scenery and no room to put it. There were ten stagehands, three dressers, and numerous actors all bumping into, and falling over, flats, chairs, Minsky headdresses, batons, rifles, flags, and, each other.

Baby June had such a quick change that while Kaye ripped off her dress (Velcro again) one of the stagehands jammed on her headdress and Mike Myers, the actor who played "Tulsa," changed Kaye's shoes. On my side of the stage, Dee Ann had a fast change, too, and we were further hampered by two chairs, two tables, one stacked upon the other, a giant rocker, Kaye Ballard, a birthday cake, and four excited small boys, also changing clothes.

It was wild.

One of the youngsters made his exit on the wrong side, got lost in the crowd, and completely missed his number. His dresser was waiting to help him change but the child never showed up. I found him on the other side the stage near tears. I told him it didn't matter. The audience didn't know whether there were supposed to be three boys or four, and it was only dress rehearsal. He cheered up, did his next number, and after the rehearsal, we got together with the boys and "choreographed" changes. They were troopers and, outside of punching each other in the nose now and then, or losing their bowties or tap shoes, they were no trouble.

It took three days to get the set and costume changes swiftly worked out. The main problem was room, or lack of it. The second was people, too many of them. Neither problem could be helped so we had to make do. We were all forced into real "togetherness" backstage. Modesty was forgotten, and no one had time to argue about anything. *Gypsy* was a successful show. The audiences loved it and never knew, I hope, what was going on behind the scenes.

Joe and I knew that in less than two weeks we had bought, borrowed, or built a hundred and one costumes, and that included hats, shoes, purses, wigs, a cow, a plaid coat for a poodle, and a strip costume that would light-up in the dark.

I've mentioned animals before. Every once in a while a script calls for a live animal. It was a prop girl's job to find the right one and take care of it during the run of the show.

Claudia, our prop girl, was a tiny, frail-looking person but a bundle of dynamic enthusiasm. She had bullied the management into giving her the job. A "no woman backstage" rule had been in effect since the theater first opened (I never quite figured out what they thought I was) but Claudia's boyfriend, Larry, was on the crew and she was determined to work there as well. She finally talked them into trying her out, did an excellent job, and was hired.

It was Claudia's job to find everything used on stage that was movable, including animals, and *Gypsy* topped the lot by calling for three—a dog, a monkey, and a lamb!

I didn't envy her.

One night, during the first act, we were alerted that Herman, the monkey, was loose. We began a frantic "monkey hunt." Herman was small and black, impossible to see him in the backstage darkness, but we could hear him. He was finally spotted, sitting on top of a piece of scenery and screaming. Luckily, the cast was singing a nice loud song and Herman's voice was just one of many. He was finally coaxed down, but not quite soon enough.

Were you there the night the *Mr. Goldstone* song was extended two measures by a shrill, unseen soprano?

G-Strings, Pasties and Paris Pants

We all thought the producers were crazy when they decided to do *Lenny*, a play about the late comedian Lenny Bruce. The off-Broadway was known as a family theater, offering light comedies and musicals. *Lenny* is, strictly speaking, a musical play, and there's comedy in it, but basically it's drama—stark, tragic, sometimes intensely shocking, about sex, drugs, nudity, not exactly family fare—but they wanted to try it on San Diego audiences.

It was the most successful play we ever did.

I hated the script. It's nothing but dialogue, none of the usual stage directions, just frank, rude language. It didn't make sense, jumped from one raw sentence to another, and didn't give me a clue as to costume requirements.

"Don't worry," I was told. "We'll have the costumes from the original show. They're coming down from LA."

Well, I'd been in this crazy business long enough to know what whenever someone said, "Don't worry," it was time to start worrying.

And I was right! Half the costumes came. The other half had been sent to San Francisco where *Lenny* was also being produced. No one had bothered to tell me that.

Seven large packing crates were carried downstairs and placed in the hall, making it a dangerous adventure to try to get in or out of the dressing rooms. One of the delivery boys handed me a four-page list, looked at me sympathetically and said,

"Well, ma'am, good luck, and please don't open them boxes until we're gone. We were there when they packed 'em." They left, leaving me slightly puzzled.

I found out what he meant when I opened the first box. There is nothing quite like the odor of old costumes that have been packed up without being cleaned. Actors sweat. They're human. They're usually nervous, and they have to perform under hot lights. These costumes had been worn for eight performances a week for months and months. They were dirty, smelly, ragged, and ugly.

Mike Phillips and I began to check the list. With over twenty people in the cast and only a week to costume the show, I had convinced the producers I needed help. They hired Mike, the same boy who'd worked in the box office earlier. He was a jewel.

An actor himself, he was able, by watching rehearsals, to make a list of who was doing what character and when they made entrances and exits. None of that was indicated in the script and, because the director had four to ten different roles, necessitating from four to ten different costumes, I was completely in the dark.

To make matters worse, they didn't rehearse in the theater, but in an old warehouse a block away. Mike spent five days running back and forth between the rehearsal hall and the theater. The director believed costumes magically fell from heaven and were altered by elves. Daily, he changed his mind about who is playing what role, and he never bothered to tell us. Every time I came back from rehearsal, I knew something would have to be changed.

Of course, we had some boxes of costumes, but not many of them were usable. Not only were they in rags, but the director had a nasty little habit of casting an actor with a 46 inch chest in a part that had formerly been played by one with a 36 inch chest. In a case like that, the only solution is to buy, borrow, or build a new costume. But it mustn't look new. Because everything was so old and moldy-looking, everything we furnished had to be old and moldy-looking, also.

The characters offered a challenge as well. We needed costumes for a Hitler, an Eichmann, an Eisenhower, four strip-tease dancers, a nurse, a cardinal, eight lepers, a pope, a judge with a robe 15 feet long, and, to top it all, the Virgin Mary, to be dressed in a G string, pasties, a long Cape, and hat trimmed with bagels! Yes, bagels. I never did find out why the director wanted those.

One of our biggest problems, literally, was a huge Dracula-like Cape. One was sent to us, but we needed another just like it. David, one of my sewing "elves," spent three days duplicating the nine-foot black and red satin thing. It was cut in pointed gores and had a high, stiffened collar that stood up in points. There were also long sticks sewn into the sides of the Cape so the actor could wave it around.

The lobby was the only place in the theater that was large enough to spread the cape out. It took two of us to pin and cut the slippery satin, and people walking by would stop and stare, probably trying to guess what we were doing on our hands knees in the lobby. After the cape was cut out, I turned it over to David. He suffered a lot, but produced a beautiful cape. He suffered even more when he watched me "grunge" it up so it would look as old as the other one.

I couldn't find any costumes for the chorus girls. I couldn't even find them on the costume list. I questioned the director.

"Oh, you'll have to make pasties and G-strings for them." He said breezily. He didn't quite snap his fingers, but gave that impression.

Well, I wasn't brought up completely stupid. I knew what pasties and G-strings were, where they were worn, and what they covered up. I just didn't have the slightest idea how to make them or how the girls were supposed to keep them on.

Then I remembered Lee. He made costumes for the theater when it was a burlesque house and now worked in the delicatessen right around the corner. If anyone could help me, Lee could. I ran to him.

"Lee, I have to make pasties and G-strings and I've never seen any."

"Don't worry, Luv, they're the easiest costumes in the world to make/. There's nothing to them."

He was right–literally. What he didn't tell me was that actresses had a bad habit. They lost their pasties. Often. No one could ever find them. I had to make dozens so I always had extras.

One night Judy Cassmore, who played Lenny's wife, lost one of her pasties on stage. Sandy Baron— Lenny— was mystified that she kept changing her blocking so her left side was never toward the audience. Then he realized what had happened and helped her "cover" her lopsided look until the end of the scene.

Georgette Rampone, always a thorn in my thimble finger, made a real fuss about wearing pasties. The G-string didn't bother her—in fact she asked me to make it smaller, I guess so she could show more—but she was convinced that gluing the pasties to her breasts would give her cancer. I finally had to get a doctor's promise that there was no danger. Even then, she used so little glue that they kept falling off.

Georgette had been with us for *Gypsy*, playing one of the strippers, and she was a nuisance. Nothing ever suited her. Her costumes were always too tight, too loose, too long, too short, or just "not quite right." She needed a different wig. She needed the wig styled in a different way. She needed more sequins on her pasties. Her strip costume wouldn't "bump" right. I soon learned to disappear when I saw her approaching. It saved unnecessary work and wear-and-tear on my disposition.

Sandy was one of the few actors who played in our theater whom I never got acquainted with. He was always polite to me, but had a habit of looking through people when they spoke to him, and you never knew if he was listening to you or not.

He insisted on a dresser of his own, and Mike was appointed, but the job consisted mainly of being in the wings with a cup of hot tea every time Sandy came offstage. Sandy seemed to like and trust him, but even Mike was often locked out of Sandy's dressing room and told to "go away."

Sometimes he was very pleasant, but he was moody, and the cast and crew were slightly afraid of his sometimes acid tongue. After quizzing me about his costumes—and thank God most of them had come in one of the boxes— Sandy left me strictly alone— until I lost his underpants.

He had informed me at our first meeting that he required a special pair of black bikini underpants. They were necessary for one of his scenes in the play. There was a pair in the costume box, but he wanted an extra pair.

"You can only get them in Paris," he informed me.

Great! The show would open in five days.

Paris yet!

I'm always cooperative.

"What are they called, Sandy, and where do I send the order?"

"I don't know. I bought 'em someplace when I was over there," he said, and trotted off to rehearsal

Well, I was tired, confused, and angry. To hell with those pants.

I had Mike bring me Sandy's fancy underpants after

every performance. I took them home and laundered them each night, and he never knew there was only one pair.

Until the last Saturday of the show.

On matinee days, I always rinsed the things out by hand and dried them in the laundromat across the street between shows. On this particular Saturday, my husband came to take me to dinner. He picked me up at the laundromat so I had Sandy's undies with me.

About ten minutes before the evening show was to begin, Mike came downstairs to get Sandy's Paris drawers.

I left them in the car.

Not only that—Don had gone to a movie, and I didn't know which one. The pants were definitely "unfindable."

Mike turned pale. "My God, what will I tell him?" He looked sick.

"I'll tell him," I said bravely. I didn't feel brave, but it was my fault.

I went up the stairs—slowly. Sandy was not known for a calm temperament.

"Sandy," I know my voice quivered. "I don't have your underpants." I explained what had happened.

"Well, I'll wear the other pair," he said.

Now I had to tell him. There wasn't another pair. No use explaining that Paris was quite a large place and across an ocean.

"Well, what am I supposed to do?" He looked at me as if I had two heads, both ugly.

Then I realized what he was wearing—not much because he'd been getting ready for the show—but what he did have on was a pair of black bikini underpants, probably from Paris.

I was mad, clear through.

"You'll get along," I snapped, and stomped downstairs to let loose behind the water heater.

Joe had introduced me to a hot glue gun during the building of *Gypsy*, but I had only watched him, never used it myself. When I found out that we had to build some "primitive" costumes for *Lenny* to match the six that arrived in one of the costume boxes, I ran out and bought a glue gun for the theater. And I'm convinced it's the only thing that enabled us to get the show costumes in time. The original primitive costumes were fantastic creations of unbleached Muslim, rope, fur, beads, burlap, feathers, and numerous other odds and ends. At first, the director was only going to use eight actors as primitives, meaning only two new costumes, but he kept adding people. Every day Mike would come back to the theater with the news that there were more primitives. We finally ended up with fourteen—plus the witch doctor —so we had to build one of those too.

Mike would run back and forth between the rehearsal warehouse and the theater all day, and spend the night in the number two dressing room surrounded by burlap, raffia, pieces of fur, wooden beads, the glue gun, and dozens of little white glue pellets. I would be working at my sewing machine, and the only sound from the dressing room would be in occasional "damn," or "shit," and I'd know he burned his fingers again. Mike had five blistered fingers on each hand by opening night, but there were fourteen primitives and a witch doctor, complete with fantastic headdresses.

I don't think I could've survived *Lenny* if it hadn't been for David Easterling.

He was a "David of all trades,"—carpenter, set designer, lighting expert, plumber. I'm convinced he could do anything. He was also tall, bearded, beautiful, and sympathetic. It was David who came downstairs at five o'clock a.m. the day we were to open and found me staring stupidly at my blistered thumb, surrounded by sequined pasties and crying.

"I'll never get finished," I howled at him. "They're impossible. They expect too much, I'm an old lady, and I should be home in my rocking chair."

I had the hiccups, and I must've been a sight. No makeup, bare feet, and glue all over me. He held me and patted me while I wept and snuffled, dampening his shirt somewhere in the vicinity of his bellybutton.

"Honey," he said, "they expect impossible things from you because you always come through. And the show will go on, too, with costumes. So put those damn little twiddlies down and get some rest. I got some more work to do, but I'll wake you at 8:00 and we'll go have breakfast."

I did, and we did, and the show did go on, with costumes.

By the third week, I still hadn't made any attempt to see *Lenny* from the front. I was too busy finishing costumes and supervising dressers to even watch the dress rehearsal. Besides, I hated the show. The dialogue I heard over the squawk boxes every night was raunchy. I knew some of the girls were practically naked and in one scene two men were completely naked. Sandy Baron was a small, unfriendly, temperamental little man, and all the costumes smelled.

Mike told me I should see it at least once.

"It's different from what you expect," he insisted. "I think you'll like it."

Not me. I had no intention of sitting through the filthy thing, and I couldn't imagine why the tickets were selling like crazy. And the audiences were not just young "freaks." Middle-aged people, senior citizens, everyone was attending our "dirty" show. They laughed, cried, sat in shocked silence, and went away either loving the play or hating it. Many of them came back again and again.

I finally decided I was being narrow-minded and silly. It wouldn't hurt to watch it once.

I sat enthralled for two hours. I forgave Sandy Baron for his coldness, his temper, even his damn French underpants. He was incredible. He was Lenny Bruce. I laughed. I cried. I listened to language that had offended me downstairs and realized that it belonged in the play. I felt drained when the performance was over, but I realized I had never once noticed what the actors were or were not wearing.

Not Blythe – No Spirit

During the three years I worked at the theater, I discovered that the most talented people are usually the most cooperative. They evidently have more self-esteem and less fear of failure. This is not always true, of course. Some of them are so used to wearing a chip on their shoulder that they can't get rid of it. Like every other theater in the world, once in a while we produced a flop, usually attributed to a poor play, poor cast, or poor director—sometimes all three.

We couldn't blame our trouble on the play this time. Noel Coward's *Blythe Spirit* has proven itself over and over. It's become a theater classic and can usually be relied upon to be successful.

Ours wasn't.

We had a well-known director, good actors, hard-working crew, and a fantastic costumer, but nothing jelled.

Lola Fisher

The director was one who's probably very competent with newcomers who are pliable and eager to please, but he was in over his head with our three strong-willed English actresses. They directed themselves, and each other. They were all very lady-like and polite, but each one knew exactly how her part would be played. Each had a "good side" and every time the director would block something, he could immediately expect,

"Oh, I do think that's a lovely bit of business, dear, but I look so much better facing the other way. All you have to do is have Lola enter from stage left instead– and a little later, too. When she comes on, she kills my laugh, and I am the star, after all."

Or,

"Now, Luv, if I sit down during that speech, Peter will completely block me when he moves down-stage. Of course, it doesn't matter to me, but for the good of the show, etc., etc."

Later in rehearsal week, things weren't quite so polite

"God dammit, I've run into that bloody chair three times. Why can't it be further up stage?"

Ann Miller was our star. Annie is a beautiful woman, and a nice one. But she believes implicitly that she is reincarnated. She attends séances—even arranged to have one at midnight in the theater. I didn't attend, but was told afterward that it had been extremely dull. The first thing she wanted to see in the theater was dressing room number four, the haunted one.

"Oh, yes," she said seriously. "I can feel the vibrations. The spirit is here." (That damned air-conditioner again).

Most actors have their idiosyncrasies, and people accept them. Annie's wouldn't have caused any problems if she hadn't decided that "dear Noel" was sending her messages. Noel Coward had been dead for several months when we started on *Blythe Spirit* and Annie insisted that some of the lines be changed because Noel had spoken to her during the night.

Even that might have been all right, but they were

never her lines, always Lucy Landau's, the actress playing Madame Arcati.

Lucy was understandably upset. Not only was it difficult for her to memorize lines, but she'd done the part many times before and always the same way. She wasn't about to change. Tempers got hotter, time got shorter, and the play got worse.

Costume-wise, it was a nightmare. The actresses not only knew exactly how their parts should be played, but also exactly what should be worn. Unhappily, no one seemed to agree on a period, not even the director. I'd been told to build one thing, and then, when it was almost done, it would have to be changed.

Lucy's outfits were the worst. The director and producer wanted her dowdy and funny. She wanted to look ladylike and pretty. And I was in the middle. I'm sure it's hard for people who aren't in show business to understand why actors are so often allowed to act like spoiled children, having temper tantrums, and making silly demands.

I think there are two reasons. First, many actors are like children – children playing dress-up, pretending to be someone else. Actors as a group are lacking in self-confidence and will do almost anything to cover it up. On the other hand, like children, they are often openly affectionate, eager to learn, and trusting. They can almost always be handled with the diplomacy—and flattery works wonders with a difficult performer.

Reason number two: even though there are always hundreds of actors out of work, it's not easy to replace someone at the last moment. It's too bad the actors are aware of this. Otherwise, they'd be a little more careful about their behavior.

The producer wanted Lucy to wear a tweed jacket and matching knickers. I agreed with him that it would be perfect for her character.

Unfortunately, Lucy had different ideas. She'd never worn knickers for the part and had no intention of starting now. She insisted on a skirt.

I didn't have time to waste waiting for them to thrash it out. Instead, I made the jacket, with matching knickers – and skirt. Then I had her try everything on, and successfully kept my face straight when she "loved" the knickers and thought they were "just the thing, dear."

Almost the same thing happened with her evening dress. She wanted an elegant, long black dress, with lots of beads around her neck. Mr. Wortman wanted her to look really funny.

Fireworks!

While they stamped and yelled at each other – Lucy threatening to quit, and Don Wortman threatening to replace her – I made an elegant long black dress and got lots of beads.

Lucy was happy. I began to add things: a ruffle, a feather in her hair, more beads, and finally a crazy sleeveless vest, with embroidery and fringe all over it. She looked like Madame Arcati should look – elegantly tacky. Everyone was happy, and her entrance in that outfit stopped the show every night.

Ann Miller

Ann Miller only had to have one costume in *Blythe Spirit*. The character she played is a ghost and the actress usually wears gray chiffon, with lots of floating panels and a hood covering her hair. Not

Annie. No, sir. She was going to be seen—her hair, her jewels, and no gray! She didn't like gray.

So she brought her own costumes, two of them. They were beautiful chiffon caftans, one white, and one gray-blue. I'm sure she paid hundreds of dollars to have them made. They were exquisitely sewn, with yards and yards of fabric. But they were both too long!

"Oh, dear," she said, "I just didn't have time to try them on before I came to San Diego. Can you please hem them up?"

Oh, sure, certainly, of course, dandy, peachy, damn!

Have you ever hand-hemmed yards and yards of expensive chiffon because your sewing machine wouldn't do anything but chew it up? Aaaagh!

She tried them on.

"They both seem to hang down on the left side, Luv," she said.

She was right. Both of those gorgeous expensive things definitely sagged to the left. Then, thank God, before I released the naughty words I was thinking, I noticed how she was standing – like a model, hand on hip and left knee bent. I asked her very sweetly to stand up straight. Magic! The hem was even.

"Well, my goodness—how about that," she said.

The white gown was fine, but the gray-blue gave me trouble. I had to exactly match the fabric to make a dress for one of the other actresses who was also a ghost. There was so much sewing to be done and such a short time—six days—that there was very little time to shop—and most of that was used up buying seven pairs of shoes before I found some to suit Lucy. I was lucky, though. I was able to find an exact match for the weird-colored chiffon. Then all I had to do was make a copy of a dress Lola already had. It was lovely—beaded, sequined, draped. The designer had probably had four weeks and three hundred dollars to work with. I had a day and a half and if I spent over twenty dollars I knew I'd get scowled at.

Well I guess you can do what you have to do. The dress looked fine—from the front. One nice thing about chiffon dresses: you can always hide your mistakes with another drape.

Blithe Spirit is a technical show. Doors open and shut by themselves, faces fly through the air, wind blows, lights go off and on. The backstage people were kept constantly busy, pushing buttons and pulling strings. We also had to lead Annie around by the hand because she had trouble with depth perception—trouble caused by an accident she'd had some time before. We also had to be careful to listen for her entrance cues because she loved to talk with the stagehands and would get involved in the conversation. One of us would grab her, hiss her opening line in her ear, and shove her onstage.

But Annie was a star. When she floated out in her white, marabou-trimmed chiffon gown, brightly made-up (she refused to wear "ghost" makeup) and dripping with jewels, the audience loved her. They were only disappointed when she didn't go into a fast tap dance.

But, the show was not good. As one reviewer wrote, "It is certainly not "blithe," and has no "spirit." The show closed a week early, but no tears from Annie. She threw a closing night party for the cast and crew. We ate pizza "with all the trimmings," drank a great deal of beer, and pretended the play had been great. With all her celestial ideas, Annie is really a down-to-earth lady and we liked her.

Hans, Was That Really You?

The play, *Norman, Is That You?* offered me some costume challenges and introduced me to a beautiful man, Hans Conried. Kind, funny to work with, and never temperamental, he was one of my particular favorites.

Hans Conried

I don't know how many dialects Hans can speak, but I loved hearing him change from one to another when he was entertaining us backstage.

When I asked him how he got started in show business, he said simply, "I needed money."

Radio needed an actor who could sound like a German officer, a French waiter, or an Italian immigrant, and Hans could.

"Once I had to do five different people on one show," he told me, "and each with a different accent."

Of course, with television that is impossible, but Hans has become well-known for the characters he created on TV series like *My Friend Irma*, *The Danny Thomas Show* and *Lost in Space*. He makes television commercials, movies, does summer stock, and TV voiceovers, where just the voice is used in a commercial or documentary.

The dialects are so good. I was surprised, upon meeting him, to discover he speaks with very little accent.

Hans wore his own clothes, with the exception of a false shirt front and tie he needed for a dream scene. After two or three trials, I managed to come up with a serviceable one. It was made from an old shirt, a lot of starch, and a bicycle clip that I inserted in the collar so he could get it on and off quickly. Hans even told me not to bother ironing his shirts.

"Just hang them up after they're washed," he said. "They'll be fine." He was an unusual man in this business. Some of the nicest ones get apoplectic over a wrinkle.

Dee Ann Johnson was also in the show. She and Fritzi each needed a fur coat. I took them to Mr. Graf's store to be fitted, and Fritzi embarrassed me terribly by announcing in a loud, hearty voice that Mr. Graf's coats, "Simply aren't chic, darling. You should see what we have in New York."

Mr. Graf was standing right there, and I wanted to die instantly. Dee Ann's mouth popped open, and I dug my elbow into her ribs to shut her up. I knew what she was likely to say if I didn't stop her.

Dee Ann is not known for either reticence or squeaky, clean language. I also knew that if I caught her eye, we'd both start laughing.

Fritzi sounded so ridiculously stuffy.

Dee Ann and I both knew she lived on unemployment compensation between shows like most actors, and had probably never been nearer to a New York fur coat than we had.

Fritzi proceeded to try on at least ten coats before she found one that "would do."

Mister Graf remained patient and gentlemanly, and as she finally decided on the right coat, he looked at me and winked.

He did understand.

I felt a lot better.

Dee Ann tried on two coats, "loved" them both, and had me choose the best one for the show. She snapped her gum, flitted her impossible eyelashes at Mr. Graf, showed her dimples to the sales lady, and ensnared them both.

Dee Ann Johnson

I worked six shows with Dee Ann. A San Diego show business personality, she's small and a little plump, with a big pouf of hair that can be improbably platinum, wildly red, or golden brown, depending on which wig she feels like wearing.

She swishes when she walks, chews gum loudly, and has a stagehand's vocabulary that she uses with a put-on Brooklyn accent. She can be funny, disgusting, sympathetic, or a bitch—whatever mood strikes her.

Dee Ann is a good performer—can sing, dance, and act—but she makes such a perfect New York prostitute that she is usually cast as a naughty, sexy, big-hearted tart.

Norman, Is That You? is a comedy about a straight-laced Jewish couple who discover their son is a homosexual. The play handles the subject humorously and tastefully, and was popular with the audience.

Jay North, (he was Dennis the Menace on television)

played Hans and Fritzi's son. (And I guess you know how we teased them about those names – they were lovingly alluded to as the Katzenjammer kids.)

Jay is a handsome, blonde young man of medium height. He furnished his own clothes. *Norman* isn't supposed to look like the preconceived homosexual man and Jay wore jeans, slacks, and "quiet" shirts. His friend, however, played by Don Sparks, must be obviously "gay." He had to have a pair of red velvet pants. Not only are red velvet trousers hard to find, they're impossible to find for a six-foot, three-inch man who's mostly legs. So, I built him a pair of gorgeous scarlet pants with flared bottoms, adding six inches to the length of the pattern. He also had to wear a robe over his clothes in one scene so I made him an incredible caftan, out of a wildly-figured print, and listened every night as the audience roared when they saw how funny he looked.

I also had to build a pair of pajamas. In one scene, Jay was supposed to wear the bottoms and Don the tops. The two actors were built so differently that ready-made pajamas wouldn't work. I made the top for Don long enough to cover what was necessary and the pants short enough for Jay so he wouldn't trip when he walked. It was a weird pair of PJ's.

During dress rehearsal, everything was going smoothly and the director suddenly exclaimed, "My God, I forgot to tell you about the sequined dress."

An interesting sentence, right? "I forgot to tell you about the sequin dress." What sequin dress?

I didn't say anything, just looked question marks at him.

"There has to be a sequin evening dress hanging in that closet," he said, "and it has to look like it would fit Don."

Well, swell! Sequin gowns for a six-foot man are even

harder to find than red velvet pants—and there wasn't any time to look, anyway. I'd have to build one.

In the depths of my despair, a small voice reminded me of an electric-blue curtain we'd made for *Anything Goes*. The fabric was beautifully glittery and looked like sequins from a short distance away. I grabbed a flashlight and a stagehand—one for light and the other to help dig—and trotted off to the dark warehouse.

The electricity had been turned off because of some squabble between landlord and tenant, and every time we needed something, we had to root around in the dark. I found the stuff under a pile of dusty junk. Part of it was water stained, but there was enough that was still usable if I cut it carefully. I got the dress finished in time for the show.

Luckily Don didn't have to wear it, so I didn't have to bother with a zipper or worry about fit. It was a long sheath with "spaghetti" straps and a diamond brooch from Woolworth's. It looked great, and got another good laugh. But, what was really fun was watching the actors' faces the first night when Hans pulled the dress out of the closet. They hadn't seen it, and it broke up the rehearsal.

I adored Hans. He told me stories about shows he had been in and actors he had worked with, brought me books and perfume, and even sang to me—on stage.

In one scene he had to change very quickly into his pajamas. The set had a little alcove that looked like the entrance to another room. Every night I would be right behind it, with Hans' pajamas ready.

As he walked toward the alcove he was supposed to hum. He did, but he always sung words under his breath, so only I could understand them. Things like, "Oh, Trina is there waiting for me, dear, dear, old girl" to the tune of Swanee River. Or, "Let me call you Trina, I'm in love with you." His lyrics weren't the greatest, but I waited each night to hear what they would be.

After the next scene, he had just a short time to get back into his suit and tie. Usually the first couple of times you do a quick change are kind of frantic. Then you get used to it, and when the ritual is set, it runs smoothly.

This change seemed to fight us. The first night I had forgotten to turn his shirt right-side-out. Quick, quick, fix it, the audience is waiting. Then I handed him his trousers backwards. The second night, he put on his shoes first—then couldn't get his pants on. But the real fun was the third night. Hans forgot to zip his fly—something I always let men do for themselves— and was well into the next scene before he knew it. He ad-libbed about being thirsty so he could go behind the alcove and zip of his trousers, leaving a slightly bewildered Jay on stage.

Later, we teased Hans, who, bless him, could always laugh at himself, and I said, in mock seriousness, "Would you like me to put *zip fly* on my list?"

He's a gentleman. He didn't quite thumb his nose at me, but the intent was there.

Pal Joe

Joe Thompkins was hired again for *Pal Joey*. In fact, he was promised four shows, for which he'd be designing sets and costumes, so he moved to San Diego, bag, baggage, and family—Rat Dog, Barnaby, and Miss Agatha.

Rat Dog, or in Joe's lingo Dawg, was aptly named, being a tiny black and white dog that closely resembled the nervous rodent. The other two were huge beautiful cats. Miss Agatha was dark gray, almost blue, and terribly aloof. Barnaby, on the other hand, was gold, mentally challenged, and loved everyone. Joe found an apartment near the theater and the four of them settled in.

I was happy to have Joe back again. He designs beautifully, is easy to get along with, and had made costuming *Gypsy* so much pleasanter.

The first week went well. Joe flew to Los Angeles to meet with our Lady Star and discuss her gowns. He showed her sketches, found out what fabrics and styles she preferred, and came back bubbling over about how nice she was.

"You'll really love her, Trina," he said. "She's just heaven!"

She was just Hell.

I don't know what happened between Joe's meeting with her and our first fitting session a week later, but whatever it was—well, let's put it this way—the "star" I met bore no resemblance to the lady he told me about.

She and a tiny, unpleasant companion strolled into the dressing room for a fitting. I had all the dresses basted and ready for her to try on. There were five gowns, all in the elegant 1930's style the script called for. They would be trimmed with sequins, fur, feathers, and "glitz," our name for fancy trim, but for now, they were covered with plastic and hanging on a rack.

She and her friend came into dressing room number two. I'm not going to use her name – I could get hung – but you've seen her. She's been singing and acting for years, and maybe that was part of the trouble. It's been a lot of years.

Anyway, in they came and, without even letting me remove the plastic bags, she refused to try on one single garment. They couldn't even see the dresses, but proceeded to devastate me with rude remarks about them.

Her friend began: "Did you tell the young man you never wear sequins?"

She hadn't.

"Oh, I couldn't possibly wear brocade, it's too shiny."

She didn't.

"That's the wrong period, dear. They never wore caftans in the '30s."

They did.

"I know you told him black crêpe. I was right there with you."

It was black crêpe. Did they mean Jersey?

Joe, help!

But Joe wasn't there. He had made an appointment for the fitting at 1:00 P.M. and it was only noon. I stood like a stump while they virtually tore the costumes, and Joe, apart.

I guess "the star" finally noticed I had gone into shock. She suddenly got sweet and apologetic. But it was too late. The battle lines had been drawn. I have an armor of silence I don now and then when things are too much for me, and I had it on now.

When they realized they weren't getting through to

me, they left.

I called Joe. I was so mad I didn't even cry—my usual reaction at such times.

Joe was stunned. "But she was so nice," he said, "and she liked all the sketches."

Well, she must have a double, then," I answered. "This one is awful, and her friend is even worse. They don't like anything!"

Joe met with our Star. She was sweet, she was apologetic, and she "knew" he was a good designer, but she was afraid he had misunderstood her wishes. Then she patted him on the head. That did it. Joe is a small man, and like most small men, hates to be patted. But he's a gentleman. He waited until he got downstairs before he exploded. He was angry about the costumes and the pat on the head, but mostly because they had come to the dressing room an hour early and jumped on me when he wasn't there.

His language was beautiful. Somehow the nastiest words sound different with a Texas drawl.

The director, John Bowab, came downstairs. He'd heard about what had happened.

"Don't let it get to you," he told us. "She's mad at me and is trying to make things difficult."

"But what about the costumes?" Joe asked. "We've only got three days."

"I've got a bunch of stuff from *Mame*," John said. "It's stored in a costume rental place in Whittier. If you can get up there, you're welcome to borrow anything you can use. They're the same period."

"What if she won't wear them?" Joe asked.

"She will," said John with a grin. Angela (Lansbury) wore them and I'll be willing to bet she'll wear anything that Angela wore."

He was right. Angela's dresses were brocade, sequins,

feathers, and fur, and she wore them and loved them.

There's a sequel to the story. The dress she liked the best was a brown velvet gown Joe had found for ten dollars in a thrift shop. He re-designed it and it was lovely. She also wore a black dress that had cost me seventy-five cents at the Goodwill store. We figured as long as she didn't know Angela hadn't worn them it would be okay, and it was.

Luckily, to offset our Lady Star, we had a man who was one of my extra favorites – Dean Jones. He was friendly, fun, easily pleased, and liked his costumes.

Dean had a lot of quick changes, and I asked him if he minded having me as a dresser, as the boys would all be too busy,

"I don't mind if you don't, honey." He laughed, and we were friends.

One thing I had to always remember

Dean Jones

was to be sure there were two sticks of gum in the pocket of every jacket or robe he wore. An important part of "Joey's" character is the way he constantly smokes. Dean had given up smoking and was afraid the play would get him started again. So, he changed the vice to gum chewing—and it worked well.

He created a real gum-chewing character, but he had to chew about ten sticks every night. We got the sugarless kind for him to protect his gorgeous white teeth, but by the end of four weeks, you'd almost gag at the sight of gum.

His closing night gift for me? A poem and a package of gum.

I never heard Dean raise his voice in anger—and he had reason to. Everything went wrong during the last few rehearsals. Props weren't where they belonged, or they fell apart when he picked them up. The stagehands were inexperienced and the scene changes were ragged. There was one drop (a piece of scenery that is let down from the "flies," the area high above the stage) that refused to hang straight. Instead of leaving it crooked and trying to fix it later, the crew worked on it during the scene, causing it to drop squarely on Dean's head. He should've yelled then. It had been a dumb thing for them to do, and painful for him. He didn't say a thing—just went to his dressing room and shut the door. I had to get the clothes for his next change and tentatively knocked on the door. I didn't know what to expect, maybe flying objects or angry words.

"Come on in." He was sitting in the chair, holding a wet paper towel over the bump on his head.

"I'm sorry. I apologize for the boys. That was a stupid accident that shouldn't have happened—how is your head?"

"Oh, I'll survive," he laughed. "That's the toughest part of me." Then he said, "They're just inexperienced, and we're all tired."

I loved him. "Have a piece of gum?" I asked. He threw the wet towel at me.

Meanwhile, Joe had been having all kinds of trouble. The head carpenter had been given a part in the show and was rehearsing every time Joe needed him. The two boys who had been hired to build sets didn't know how to read the scene design plans so Joe had to be at the warehouse constantly. Also, even though they were being paid $6.50 an hour, if someone didn't stand over them, they would just take off whenever it suited them. They didn't seem to realize, or maybe just didn't care, that Joe couldn't paint the flats until they were built.

It was a good thing that Joe and I worked together before, because he had to trust me to go ahead with things when he wasn't around to give his okay. Thank goodness he made all the sketches and we'd done most of the shopping early, because supervising the set building and painting everything was a full-time job—and then some. He had one helper, Gail Bruce, and should've had at least three.

Gail and another apprentice, Denise Drennen, had come to us when we were starting *Lenny.*

The theater management had decided to start an apprentice program to save money. There weren't a lot of applicants because, although there are dozens of kids interested in theater, there are very few who can afford to put in the amount of time theater work demands from unpaid apprentices. Gail and Denise were college students, majoring in theater arts, and would get credit for their summer work. They were both gems. They could both sew reasonably well, but Gail was more interested in working on the sets, so she helped Joe while Denise worked with me.

Those two willing slaves painted, sewed, shopped, ran errands, ironed, made tea and kept Joe and me from disintegrating They were hard workers, loyal to us, and stayed constantly cheerful. They were both willing to work all night, if necessary, and sometimes did.

The two girls were as different as you could imagine. Denise was a blonde, plump, energetic, and so enthusiastic about everything that you expected her to explode. Gail was small and slim, with long, dark hair and was always so quiet you forgot she was around. Between them they did the work of six people and earned our eternal love and gratitude.

The costumes we borrowed for the star were expensively and beautifully made, but there was one that was absolutely wrong. It was a peach-colored chiffon negligee trimmed with feathers. It not only looked awful on the lady, but destroyed the color coordination Joe had planned for the scene. We both hated it, but she liked the fussy thing and insisted upon wearing it. Poor Joe had to stand by and see his whole concept of the scene spoiled by what he called "the chicken-feather shit." The negligee was molting, and every night the stage had to be swept after the scene.

Our favorite gift on closing night was a doll given to us by the prop girl, Georgia Vojlko. She had made a ragdoll with the hair and features of our star. It was dressed in peach chiffon trimmed with the swept-up feathers, and had long pins for voodoo purposes.

There was one scene in *Pal Joey* that really took ingenuity to costume. It was the ballet scene, which wasn't a ballet at all, but rather a parade of famous old stars.

We needed costumes for Jean Harlow, Shirley Temple, Laurel and Hardy, Count Dracula, May West, Pavlova and the Nijinski, Charlie Chaplin, Carmen Miranda, and Greta Garbo. The director didn't make up his mind to use the ballet until the last minute. It's often left out of the show, probably because it creates such a costume problem. After changing his mind three times, he decided to do it—and he wanted it costumed all in black, white, and silver! Whoopee!! Can you imagine how that bit of news struck us at 11:00 P.M.., two days before opening?

I won't bore you with how we accomplished it. We did, and it looked good, but we were saved by the fact that the whole scene was lit by a "strobe" light that flickered constantly, making the scene look likes an old movie. It was great for us because it effectively hid numerous safety pins, large basting stitches, and even staples.

One nice thing about the ballet scene was that it utilized the talents of some of our backstage people. Claudia played Shirley Temple, Larry played Stan Laurel, and Mike Phillips was Chaplin. Mike was also used as a dancer, and Claudia and Larry had speaking roles. They were all good, too, and we were glad they finally had a chance to perform.

On the day before opening, Joe lost his temper. And did he ever! I could always tell when Joe was angry. I had learned to read the signs: the short, stabbing puffs on the cigarette, the twitching muscle in his jaw. He seldom let his feelings show, however, and always seemed calm and quiet.

The day had started badly. We were all tired and cranky from tension, overwork, and lack of sleep. We were sewing in the corner of the warehouse where the sets were built because we'd run out of space in the theater. There were too many people in the cast. Also, the halls were crowded with the seven boxes of *Lenny* costumes that we'd been told to pack for the Chicago show. The boxes had been sitting there for nine days. Joe had asked over and over again to have them moved so we'd have room for the finished costumes for *Pal Joey*.

There they sat.

We were gathered around my cutting table listening to Joe explain how he wanted May West's dress when Fred came into the warehouse.

"Hey," he said. "Mr. Wortman wants you to get those boxes out of the downstairs. He says it's too crowded down there."

There was a dead silence. Mr. Wortman wanted us to

move seven huge packing crates? As if we didn't have anything else to do? No one could think of anything to say.

Suddenly Joe, our quiet, unflappable Joe, picked up my best pair of scissors, stabbed them into the table with all his force, and blew up.

"God dammit, that's the final straw!" he yelled, and took off for the theater at top speed.

There was another dead silence. Fred stood like he'd been turned to stone. The girls looks stunned, stupefied. I started to laugh. I couldn't help it. I sat down and laughed until I cried. Joe, our nice quiet Joe, had finally let loose.

When I could finally speak coherently, I assured everyone that it was the best thing that could have happened.

"He should have blown his top three days ago," I said. "He's been working without enough sleep, without enough help, and without enough money. He'll feel better, now, and if he stays mad until he gets to the theater, I bet it'll do some good. They've never seen him lose his temper either."

Half an hour later, Joe stuck his head in the door and grinned at us. "Did I scare anybody?"

"I hope you stayed mad long enough to do some good," I said.

He looked sheepish. "Ya know what? I charged over there with all my adrenaline pumpin', all ready for a rip-snorten' whandoodle—and nobody was there." He looked so dejected we couldn't help laughing. He laughed with us. "Okay, ladies, I've had my tantrum for today. Let's get to workin'."

And you know what? It did help. Mike had been in the warehouse practicing and had heard the whole thing. I don't know who he talked to, but two hours later the boxes had all been moved out of the downstairs hall. It had been a small war, but we'd won.

No one was unhappy when *Pal Joey* closed. It would've been a successful show, with good audiences, but there was tension and unpleasantness backstage. Closing night, however, was fun. Because everyone was so relieved that it was nearly over, there was a feeling of togetherness that hadn't been there before.

Every night Georgia and I helped Dean with a very quick change. It took two of us, and was done in the wings. He always teased us and made remarks about his two "beautiful dolls." Beautiful? Sure. We usually wore jeans, comfortable shirts, and tennis shoes, or no shoes at all. On closing night when he came dashing off stage, he found his "beautiful dolls" dressed in evening gowns, high heels, and dangling earrings. He hardly recognized us, and we were warmed by his heart felt "Wow."

Dean played tricks on everyone that night. He even ad-libbed in a scene with the leading lady and made her laugh. She got even, though. In the last scene "Joey" is alone on stage. He's been knocked unconscious by the "bad guys" and his "lady friend" off stage calls to him,

"Are you all right now?"

"I'm okay. Did they get the money?" he answered.

"No," she was supposed to answer, and then explain how she kept it from them.

But on that last night of the play, she answered, "Yes."

Just "yes" made Dean's next lines completely useless, and he had to try and ad-lib his way out of it. The audience caught on and everyone had fun.

It even made *me* like her a little better.

Exit

I worked at the off-Broadway theater for nearly three years, costuming twenty-six shows. I met hundreds of interesting people, and learned a great deal about show business, show people, and me. After twenty-six shows, all successful as far as the costuming was concerned, I still broke into a chilly sweat upon meeting new people. I still worried about each new challenge. My sewing machine still suffered occasionally from hiccups, and I still wept when I was tired and anyone looked at me crookedly. I guess some of us don't change.

However, upon looking back, I wouldn't exchange those years for anything in the world. I worked hard, true, but was always treated with respect and affection by the people I worked for and with. Many of the actors caused me problems, usually because they had problems of their own, but for the most part they were nice people—with a little more talent than the rest of us.

Not only do I have a whole wall of autographed pictures, and many, many lovely gifts that remind me of the givers, I also have a heart full of warm memories.

I remember my going away party the cast and crew of *Mister Roberts* gave me. My husband Don and I were going to Europe and the show would be over when I got back. There was a cake, cards, hugs, wine, and best wishes. Even though I was excited about the trip, it was hard to leave so many friends, especially knowing I probably wouldn't see any of the cast again. We got to the airport early the next morning. There, waiting to see us off, were Gordon and John, who were playing Doc and the Captain in the show. Actors hate to get up early in the morning and I was so touched I wept all over the box of chocolates they gave me.

I remember sitting in the number two dressing room with Arlene Golonka, and Elizabeth Allen, both such beautiful people, gossiping as we sewed, like housewives at a coffee klatch.

It was during the run of *Who's Afraid of Virginia Woolf*, a show I haven't written about because it wasn't a busy show for me. There were just four people in the cast and only one costume change. The actors were all professional and the show went so smoothly that, except for my having to learn to tie a man's necktie when Carl Betts injured his hand, there wasn't a lot to do.

Poor Carl. He had to perform the whole last week with his left hand in a cast. And I know he hated to have me practically dress him. He never let his impatience show, though, as I fumbled with his necktie and shirt buttons.

Learning to tie a necktie on someone else came in handy later. One night during *Pal Joey* I was helping Dean Jones with a quick change. He always tied his own tie, but that night, after trying twice, he suddenly said shakily, "Trina, you'll have to tie this. You know how?"

Yes, thank God, I did.

Later he said, "I never had that happen before. I just suddenly could not tie my tie. Nervousness, I guess. Thanks."

I felt useful and appreciated.

I remember Gavin was the only actor who performed at our theater

Gavin McLeod

who made me cry, every night. There's a scene, a poignant moment in the play, but somehow Gavin seemed to live it. He even had his back to the audience as he walked away, but those of us standing off stage could see his face. It got me every night. Besides, I loved him. Gavin was sweet, easy to get along with, fun, and he dressed in number four every night with no ill effects (except being chilled by the air conditioner).

I remember the changeover nights. We always had to work all night to get the old show "struck" and the new one ready. Around midnight our bosses would send out for giant pizzas, beer, and soft drinks. Pizza has to be the worst thing in the world to throw into a tired, empty stomach, but somehow it never bothered us. Maybe the indigestible stuff was counteracted by the camaraderie of a dozen exhausted, dirty crew members sprawled on the stage or in the two front rows of the small theater. We told jokes, sang bawdy songs, and relaxed for a while. Feuds and hard feelings were forgotten as we pulled ourselves together for the frantically busy time ahead.

And somehow, no matter what, the show always went on.

THE PLAYS

THE PLAYERS

Made in the USA
San Bernardino, CA
22 November 2015